AMERICAN CREDOS

BOOKS BY STUART CHASE

AMERICAN CREDOS
LIVE AND LET LIVE
SOME THINGS WORTH KNOWING
GUIDES TO STRAIGHT THINKING
THE PROPER STUDY OF MANKIND
POWER OF WORDS
ROADS TO AGREEMENT
DEMOCRACY UNDER PRESSURE
WHERE'S THE MONEY COMING FROM?
THE TYRANNY OF WORDS
RICH LAND, POOR LAND
A NEW DEAL
THE ECONOMY OF ABUNDANCE
MEXICO
MEN AND MACHINES
YOUR MONEY'S WORTH (with F. J. Schlink)
THE TRAGEDY OF WASTE

AMERICAN CREDOS

by Stuart Chase

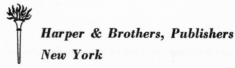

Harper & Brothers, Publishers
New York

CONTENTS

71·128

FOREWORD

In any serious discussion of large issues, domestic or foreign, somebody is sure to say that the American people are behind this policy, or will never stand for that policy. How does the speaker know what the American people will stand for? Mostly he does not know. Often he assumes, humanly enough, that the American people stand with him.

I have doubtless made such assumptions during hot discussions in the past. In this book, however, I am letting the American people speak for themselves. In this book, except for some personal observations in the last chapter, I am trying to keep my predilections out of it.

I have compiled the testimony of the polls to show what Americans believe about many important issues. I have also tried to assess, from the same source, the areas of their ignorance, in the hope that some of the blind spots may be illuminated.

The Fund for the Republic in recent years has been holding a series of lively and often profound discussions on such matters as the American economy, the status of large corporations, labor unions, politics, the mass media, the law, foreign affairs. The officials of the Fund, remem-

bering a report I had made on the young science of opinion research in *The Proper Study of Mankind,* asked me
to get together some poll figures bearing upon the discussion subjects, as a check against overenthusiastic generalizations. I did so, and my report was circulated internally
by the Fund, possibly with benefit to discussion members.

The idea has now been considerably expanded. I am
grateful to the Fund for steering me in this direction, and
I hope the larger study will be of some use to a wider
audience. I also hope that foreign observers of the American scene will look into it, and gain a clearer view of
what the American people believe. In Russia in the summer of 1961, talking to cultural leaders at a joint conference, I found their picture of America dim and distorted.
I wish that we had a comparable analysis of Russian mass
opinion to correct our own distortions.

I am grateful to my wife, Marian, for devoted editorial
labor and sound advice. I am grateful to Evan Thomas
and Genevieve Young at Harpers, to Elmo and Burns
Roper, and to Professor Philip Hastings at Williams College, for reading the manuscript, in whole or in part, and
contributing many helpful suggestions. I am grateful to
my conscientious secretarial assistants, Christine Loring
and Lola Donnell.

The reader will not find sources in the text, but only
small numbers which are keyed to sources, chapter by
chapter, in the Appendix.

STUART CHASE

Redding, Connecticut
January, 1962

AMERICAN CREDOS

1
GROWTH OF A SCIENCE

Public opinion is important in every society. Absolute monarchs, dictators, czars, and commissars have been forced to allow for it, or at some point face revolution. It is particularly important in a democracy, where people elect their political leaders and sometimes bring strong pressure on them to follow certain policies.

What do the people want? How deeply do they want it, and how long will they continue to want it? How much attention should a leader pay to a given public demand? For the wise and vigorous democratic leader the voice of the people may not be the voice of God, but it is not something to be disregarded. Popular demands and beliefs should be known, and allowed for in plans for action.

Yet no civilized society, since the first cities arose in Mesopotamia five thousand years ago, has ever, until very recently, had a way to measure the wants and feelings of the people with reasonable accuracy. History might be a different story if such a technique had been available to Pericles, say, or Caesar, George III, Louis XVI, Woodrow Wilson, or Nicholas II.

A leader must understand his people to some degree at least, or they will not follow him. Also, a nation, like an individual, should have some understanding of its own character. How does it differ from that of other nations, and what forces have molded it? "National character" is a slippery term from the semantic viewpoint, but the modern science of anthropology can find consistent and predictable modes of behavior and belief in one society, and compare them with those of other societies. Behavior patterns, character, belief systems, all are parts of the same culture. Public opinion is close to its vital center, but in some ways the hardest to handle because of its volatility. Any tool is useful that helps us to explain and understand a culture—especially our own, which being nearest is sometimes least visible.

Many critics distrust and discount the effort to measure public opinion scientifically. Often enough, the same skeptics who downgrade opinion polls do not hesitate to generalize about national character and desires with dogmatic finality, their tools being intuition, random observation, and projection of their own necessarily limited experience. "The American people will never consent," they say. Or, to quote a prominent commentator in the Berlin crisis of 1961: "The vast majority of U.S. citizens remain resolved to face Communist pressure without yielding an inch." How does he know?

Public opinion research has been developed largely in the United States, where opinion is conspicuously potent, and often inflated by the commercial efforts of the mass media. Let us examine the way the research tools have been developed.

TOOLMAKERS

Up to a generation ago, the best America (or any country, for that matter) could do to measure opinion was represented on the one hand by sidewalk surveys, and on the other by mail questionnaires—for example, the postcard presidential polls of the *Literary Digest*.

As far back as 1824, a newspaper in Harrisburg, Pennsylvania, sent out reporters to ask pedestrians whether they intended to vote for Henry Clay, Andrew Jackson, John Quincy Adams, or William H. Crawford for President. The paper tabulated and published the answers. Thereafter, many newspapers followed suit, and some still do. There is no certainty, however, that people on the street at a given time represent a true sample of public opinion in that town, let alone in the nation. Sidewalk surveys are subject to serious bias.

The *Literary Digest* in the 1920's undertook to sample the whole nation by mailing return post cards to citizens. Returns were published state by state, and for the United States as a whole. As many as 20 million cards were sent out on a single ballot, and produced up to three million returns. The *Digest* did not fare too badly in earlier presidential elections, but 1936 was an unmitigated disaster. The magazine elected Landon comfortably, while the voters elected Roosevelt. In due course, the *Digest* retired from the magazine field.

BIAS, THE CORRUPTER

What was the trouble? Bias was the trouble. Opinion surveys are always in trouble when bias * enters—unless the surveyor is specifically trying to measure bias. The respondents who returned the *Literary Digest* post cards were a biased selection for two formidable reasons. First, the cards were sent to lists of telephone subscribers, automobile owners, et cetera—people who had somewhat higher incomes than the rank and file in those years. Second, citizens with superior education were more likely to fill out the card and mail it back. White collars are handier with a pen than blue collars—or were at that time. Republicans tend to have higher incomes and more schooling than Democrats, and so the post cards showed that the Republican candidate was in—until the actual vote showed the opposite.

Bias is the nightmare of the poll takers. The best way it can be banished in a mail survey—or at least reduced to negligible percentages—is to limit the inquiry to people of similar background. Thus a mail survey of members of the American Economics Association asking what they think of a certain book on economics—such as J. K. Galbraith's *Affluent Society*—will not produce too much bias.** If enough careful attention is given to a mail survey, including follow-up mailings, bias can be kept at a minimum.

---

* Bias here means a sample that does not correspond to the whole, or "universe," it purports to represent.

** This has been done. About half of the respondents thought it a good book.

Later we shall look at various other dangers and biases which analysts must avoid.

SAMPLING THEORY

The motive behind scientific sampling is simple economy. If an inspection of 10 units will give the same result as an inspection of all the 100 units in a given "universe," the cost of the inspection is cut way down, in terms of either money or man hours.

Sampling as a scientific and practical technique is hundreds of years old. Inventories of grain, fluids, merchandise have long been calculated by sampling. The total population of a country has been estimated by counts in sample communities. As a writer I frequently use elementary sampling theory to estimate how many words I have written on a given assignment. I know, within two or three percent, and without complete counting, how many words are in the manuscript of this book. I carefully count the words on 10 pages selected at random, average them, and multiply by the number of pages written. The total will be close enough for my purposes and those of my publisher. Observe also that a 50-page count will not be much more accurate than a 10-page count. The *Literary Digest* took a sample, but it was not an accurate sample because of bias. Actually, the same percentage of inaccuracy could probably have been achieved by sending out a million post cards rather than 20 million—which would have saved a lot of printing and mailing.

Scientific sampling theory was first applied to public opinion in the 1920's as an experiment in the field of marketing research. Such questions as: "Do you like our Z-point toaster?" were asked of a sample of consumers, as reflecting the opinion of a "universe" of possible buyers. Various advertising agencies also experimented with this technique and found that it paid off in sales.

THE EARLY YEARS

In *Fortune* magazine for July, 1935, the firm of Cherington, Roper and Wood (later to become Elmo Roper and Associates) published the results of the first survey of public opinion based on scientific sampling. Three months later, in October, 1935, Dr. George Gallup released a survey of public opinion to Sunday newspapers. Both poll takers employed trained interviewers to ask a sample of Americans what they thought about Mr. Roosevelt, the New Deal, and other public issues. The sample followed the quota method, and, within calculated margins of error, was thought to reflect the opinion of a universe comprehending all adult Americans.*

Questions in this pioneer period usually required a simple choice between opposites. "Do you approve of the Civilian Conservation Corps? Answer Yes or No." Presently the critical importance of the "Don't Knows" (D.K.'s) was discovered. Many respondents had never heard of the Civilian Conservation Corps. From then on D.K.'s were treated with increasing respect as an index of public indifference or plain ignorance.

"Cafeteria" questions were then introduced, where respondents were asked to select one answer from a range

* See page 30 for description of a quota sample.

of choices on the counter. If the subject was Mr. Roosevelt's performance, replies were arranged like this:

> Do you highly approve?
> Mildly approve?
> Mildly disapprove?
> Highly disapprove?
> No opinion (D.K.)

Sometimes as many as six alternatives were offered, not
necessarily showing the intensity of the respondent's feeling.

Multiple questions were offered in a variant of the
cafeteria method—a technique called "scaling." For a poll
on race prejudice, for instance, at one end of the scale
would be the question: "Do you favor the complete segregation of the races?" At the other end: "Do you approve
of mixed marriages?" In between would be questions dealing with desegregation in big league baseball, public housing, employment, public schools, and so on—all in scale
between the two extremes.*

As the new discipline developed, with more and more
demand from businessmen, government, universities,
newspapers, plain citizens, the original experts in statistics
were joined by representatives of other social sciences—
economists, political scientists, sociologists, psychologists,
anthropologists. Compilation of results was entrusted to
punch cards and high-speed tabulating machines. Probability mathematics was brought into play.

---

* The technique was advanced by the work of E. S. Bogardus, and
is sometimes known as the "Bogardus social distance scale."

AROUND THE WORLD

Opinion research is now a massive enterprise, with agencies all around the world. The British were in the field almost as early as the Americans, and developed a special technique called "mass observation," in which members of the research staff *listen* to live conversations at carefully chosen spots—in pubs, buses, and other public places—on selected public issues, say, banning the H-bomb. In the United States there are now more than a score of responsible polling organizations, some in universities, some in government, some private.

The Roper Public Opinion Research Center at Williams College acts as a clearinghouse to collect, classify, and permanently file significant results. For a modest fee, you may obtain these results on any subject which has ever been responsibly polled, including figures from 18 American agencies and 26 foreign polling agencies, serving 21 countries in the so-called free world. The Center has a new building under construction now in 1962.

Not to be outdone by the West, Russia in 1960 set up the Soviet Public Opinion Institute, which prepares questionnaires for citizens to answer.[1]* *Pravda*, on January 6, 1961, reported a set of 12 questions addressed to young Russians from 15 to 28 years of age, including: "Do you personally have a purpose in life?" and, "Have young people, from your viewpoint, negative features?" Most authorities have thought that scientific polling would be impossible behind the Iron Curtain because of the tight

* Superior figures refer to notes in the Appendix of Sources.

control of opinion, though perhaps certain kinds of opinion could be collected with interesting and revealing results. But if the above questions are a fair sample, it is obvious that the Russians have a good deal to learn about scientific polling. They have yet to master the principles of Step 1—the semantics of the question—to be described in detail in the next chapter.

USES OF THE POLLS

The demand for measuring public opinion is enormous and growing. Most of us still tend to identify polling with political elections, but this is only a tiny corner of the whole field. By far the largest area is that of market research, which collects data that almost never reach the public. Here is an analysis of the time spent by one large research organization over the 10 years, 1950 to 1960:

	Percent of time
Consumer use and demand, brand image	29
Product and package design	13
Advertising effectiveness	8
Analysis of mass media	7
Corporate public relations, employee relations, corporate image	15
Political studies (including elections)	13
Other public affairs, social issues, etc.	12
Miscellaneous surveys	3
Total work of agency	100

From the above it appears that the great majority of all opinion surveys in this agency are taken on behalf of commercial clients. Such clients, we may be sure, do not spend good money year after year for nothing. They have sound reason in their sales sheets to trust the sampling technique.

Other polling organizations, such as university and government bureaus, collect data principally on social and economic issues. Take, for instance, the work of the U.S. Labor Department on unemployment. Each month, field interviewers check 35,000 households in 333 areas throughout the country. Today, in 1962, there are upward of 50 million households in the United States, and so the sample includes about one household in 1,500. From this monthly sample, total unemployment is calculated—a figure of tremendous national importance. Surveys of health, of crime, youth surveys, are often based on sampling theory. The Bureau of the Census uses it constantly and thereby saves taxpayers enormous sums. The Public Health Service recently estimated the effects of smoking by sampling theory. The U.S. Information Agency uses polls abroad to determine foreign reactions to American policies and American behavior.

SURVEYS DURING THE WAR

Opinion research and scientific sampling had vital applications during World War II. Studies were made to determine housing facilities, goods in short supply, dealer inventories, over-all consumer wants, public reaction to war measures, characteristics of selectees, attitudes of workers in war plants, radio listening habits. These manifold activities caused poll taker Angus Campbell to say at the end of the war: "The science of sampling has reached the point where it can select unbiased samples, of known probable error, to represent virtually any universe a surveyor is interested in." [2]

Samples include matters of fact or of opinion. The former are represented by a sample indicating total unemployment, the latter by a sample showing respondents' feelings about labor unions. The reader will find more illustrations of opinion in this book, as being nearer to the idea of a credo.

The late Dr. Samuel A. Stouffer, working for the Army, polled G.I.'s about their food, their equipment and uniforms, the entertainment offered, promotion methods, leadership, discipline, and "What are your plans after the war?" [3] A scientific sample of soldiers themselves determined the "point" system of discharge, with the result that approval for the system never fell below 70 percent. Because of Stouffer's work, the Army knew in advance, and within three percent, how many claimants there would be under the G.I. Bill of Rights—a finding which saved the Treasury millions of dollars.

Stouffer's corps of interviewers once put the following question to soldiers: "Is an enlisted man more concerned with what other enlisted men think of him than with what his officers think?" The "Yes" vote was 89 percent. Even officers voted 78 percent "Yes." As a result, the Army worked to solidify group loyalty—"Don't let your buddies down"—rather than blind loyalty to officers.

Rensis Likert, now of the University of Michigan, using sampling theory, found that if the U.S. Treasury made it easier to cash in war bonds, more new bonds would be bought by citizens, and more bonds *net* would stay bought. The finding was contrary to positive opinion in high quarters. But the Treasury trusted the poll and adopted the new method, "with the results predicted."

The Office of Price Control kept in close touch with the public by frequent opinion surveys. If a poll showed public resentment in St. Louis, say, trouble shooters were rushed to the city before the grievance could "escalate," in the graphic new term. Sometimes a ruling was changed, sometimes a better explanation was given. In June of 1946, a poll showed that 78 percent of Americans wanted price controls continued for a while. Congress, however, killed the controls, in the mistaken belief that free competition would keep prices in line. The people were wiser than Congress.

Once a poll stopped a race riot. A postwar housing project in Seattle had 300 Negro families and 700 white. Incidents occurred, tension mounted, violence seemed imminent. The Public Opinion Laboratory of the University of Washington, under Dr. Stuart Dodd, rushed 25 trained interviewers to the scene. A sampling of residents' attitudes showed little real race antagonism, but acute dissatisfaction with cold houses, bad kitchen equipment, terrible interior roads. Equipment and roads were repaired, and race tension faded out.

Surveys are now conducted in shop and office to find

out how workers feel about the boss, the union, the company, and how well they like their jobs. Elmo Roper tells about asking workers a series of such questions in a Standard Oil refinery. The men were naturally suspicious, but when Roper, at a union meeting, guaranteed that no names would be revealed, and that union as well as management would see the results, the atmosphere began to ease. Finally the union president got to his feet.

"I'm for it," he said, "and here's why. I tell management what the workers want. They want this and they want that, and I bang the table! So Bill here [the superintendent of the refinery, who was present], Bill says no, they want that and they want this, and he bangs the table! But neither of us knows a damn thing about what you fellows want, and I'm for Mr. Roper finding out."

Nobody knows what the American people really want, failing a dependable method to measure it. Biologists and psychologists can tell us much about the built-in drives of the human organism. Anthropologists can tell us much about the patterns imposed by the culture. But only direct quantitative research can tell us how people are reacting to current issues, what they think about their leaders, the relative strength of some of their hopes and fears. Only scientific research can puncture the glib generalizations, beloved of table pounders, about people in the mass.

Political wiseacres were stunned when Nelson Rockefeller decided not to seek the nomination for President in 1960 because opinion surveys indicated that his chances were not bright. This demonstrates, of course, not so much the function of the polls in the public interest, as the reliance now being put in their technical competence.

The poll takers have had a difficult time living down what happened in the presidential campaign of 1948, a disaster almost rivaling that of the *Literary Digest* in 1936. Most of them announced that Mr. Dewey was elected, some weeks before voters went to the booths in November to elect Mr. Truman. Careful students have long been skeptical of the utility of polls for political candidates, on the ground, among others, of creating a "band wagon" effect. If the opinion polls show candidate Jones far ahead, some citizens, it is alleged, will be inclined to vote for a sure winner, while citizens opposed to Jones, giving up the battle, may stay home.

There is one great technical advantage in political polling. The analysts take a sample before election and apply it to the universe of all voters. After election, by comparing actual results with predicted results, the research man knows how well his technical methods are working, and can take steps to improve them. It is confirmation by experiment as in a chemical laboratory.

The scientific surveyors did far better than the *Literary Digest* in 1936, predicting Roosevelt's election without trouble. They predicted it, with ample margin, again in 1940 and 1944. But in 1948 they predicted Dewey and received a devastating setback. What was the matter? The chief trouble seems to have been that they were not sufficiently aware of the now-established fact that campaigns or outside events can change voters' opinions in the last few weeks. In the case of Roosevelt, most voters made their minds up early, but Dewey and Truman had more uncertain public images. News events in October, affecting both labor and farmer, apparently threw a substantial bloc of last-minute votes to Mr. Truman. Had the election taken place in early September of 1948—when the pollsters began to publish their confident predictions —Dewey might have won. Incidentally, if the "bandwagon" argument had any substantial validity, Truman would not only have lost, but lost by a larger vote than the September polls indicated.

Not only presidential predictions have been scrutinized and analyzed since the debacle of 1948, but the whole polling process. Some recent improvements will appear in the next chapter. The poll takers were very guarded in their 1952 and 1956 predictions, but the wide popularity of General Eisenhower as a war hero made prediction not too difficult. The election of 1960, however, presented a problem, with such unknown factors as the effect of Mr. Kennedy's Catholicism, and Mr. Nixon's unpopularity in liberal and labor quarters. It is instructive, I think, to note how well the poll takers had learned the lesson of 1948.

The finger-in-the-wind commentators came swinging out, toward the end of the 1960 campaign, for a Kennedy landslide! The opinion polls showed nothing of the kind; it was the closest thing in years. Said Roper: "This is the most volatile election we have ever tried to measure, and it could go either way." The big national agencies reported a hairline finish. When the actual count was completed, all were found well within the computable margin of error. Kennedy won over Nixon, as all the world knows, by only 200,000 popular votes.

The West German elections of 1961 also indicate the reliability of polling techniques. Here is a comparison between the figures of Gallup's German agency predicting the election, and the actual vote: [4]

	Gallup's EMNID	Actual vote
Christian Democrats	46%	45.3%
Social Democrats	38	36.3
Free Democrats	10	12.7
Others	6	5.7
	100	100.0

Angus Campbell summed the situation up: "Just as the polls were not as bad as they looked in 1948, they are probably not as good as they look in 1960. . . . The hazards of predicting have certainly not been eliminated, but they have been reduced."

Although we shall be primarily concerned with *issues* rather than elections in the pages to come, recent election results help to give us confidence in the techniques now being used.

2
MEASURING OPINION

The Eight Steps

Eight well-defined steps must be taken in a dependable survey of public opinion. Each step requires rigorous technical attention. Let us examine them briefly, as background for the chapters and figures to come.

STEP 1. ANALYZING THE ISSUE

As a research man, you are seeking to determine opinion about a given public issue—the work of UNESCO, perhaps, or minimum wages, or the advisability of installment debt. This immediately raises the problem of what constitutes an "opinion"—at least one worth measuring. The first step, accordingly, is to scrutinize carefully the issue and the questions bearing on it.

A sample of American adults, says psychologist Hadley Cantril, cannot be expected to have a full set of opinions on the same issue. A valid opinion held by an individual is built up from past experience, usually as a guide to action. If no action is contemplated, the opinion will be less dependable. Opinion does not change, says Cantril, unless the purpose of the respondent changes. If the respondent believes that the President is "doing a good job," thereby relieving the respondent of worrying about public issues himself, he will continue to support the President as long as he wishes to be relieved of the responsibility. But if the President should lead the country into a military crisis over Berlin, let us say, and if the respondent feared that he might be drafted, his opinion of the President's stewardship might rapidly shift.

When public information on an issue is scanty, and opinions are lightly held, a respondent can be pushed into adopting about any point of view.[1] Thus, when people were told by poll takers in the 1930's that Roosevelt approved a given program, mass approval was likely to show a high percentage, even if respondents were largely ignorant of the issue. Apparently they felt that Papa knows best.

Again, if the issue touches the standard belief systems of the culture, we can expect high support for the conventionally approved thing to do, even if the respondent does not do it. If we ask: "Did you vote in the last election?" experience has shown that the percentage of yeses in the sample will exceed the percentage of actual to potential voters, in that particular election. Why? Because voting in the American democracy is the right thing to do. There will be practically 100 percent agreement, in any opinion survey, that husbands should be faithful to their wives. But it would be unwise to conclude that respondents' conduct always corresponds to their answers. Adultery is not something invented by writers of novels.

Paul Coates, of the Los Angeles *Mirror-News*, ran a simple popular test in 1959, to evaluate respondents' background information and their suggestibility. He called 150 names at random from the telephone book and asked them: "Do you think the Mann Act helps or deters the cause of organized labor, and should it be repealed?" Most of the calls were answered by housewives. Only 12 percent properly identified the Mann Act, which prohibits "white slave" traffic across state lines. Thirty-eight percent, however, favored repeal of the Act. "We're strictly against that Act in our family," said one lady. "It certainly shouldn't be repealed," said another, "Hoffa gets away with too much as it is."

The Coates experiment illustrates a constant danger in measuring opinion. Most of us dislike admitting our ignorance. If we know nothing about an issue, we sometimes pretend that we do, and so protect our egos. The question to be asked on a poll, accordingly, needs to be widely understood, or else it should be preceded by a question to determine the respondent's knowledge. More research is needed on the validity of opinion and its motivation; Cantril's shrewd analysis should be further developed.

STEP 2. SELECTING THE "UNIVERSE"

To what universe shall we direct our question? Shall it be all adult Americans, or sharecroppers in Alabama, property owners in Connecticut, college undergraduates, potential buyers of washing machines, or what? Questions

about the influence of Greek dramatists on English literature might well be asked of professors of literature, but
not of Chicago taxi drivers. Research agencies, now established in a score of countries as we have seen, can ask
the same question of similar "universes" all over the
world, for instance: "What do you think of the United
Nations' performance in the Congo?"

STEP 3. SELECTING THE SAMPLE

Here our research can become very technical. Shall we
use the "quota," the "random," or the "panel" method?
The first was an early favorite, but is now giving way to
the random method, based on more rigorous probability
mathematics.

In the quota method, the researcher sets up "clusters"
in the sample which he hopes will closely agree with
clusters in the universe. He selects the same proportion of
men and women, rich and poor, educated and unedu-
cated, whites and Negroes, city folks and rural folks,
young and old, and so on.

The pure random method depends on some automatic
way of choosing, which gives each individual in the universe an equal chance of being included in the sample.
Suppose we want to know the percentage of members in
a given service club who go to church regularly. Here is
the club's card file, listing, say, 40,000 members. Now
pick up a book, any book, and open it at random. If the
page is 73, take 3, the low digit. Good, we will begin our
survey with the *third* card in the file, and take every hun-
dredth card thereafter. If we want a larger sample, we

take more names—say, every twentieth card.

In a nation-wide survey of adults, the poll takers now normally use what they call a "modified random sample." Perhaps 150 regions or counties across the United States will be chosen by random methods; then subareas, like city blocks, or rural villages, will be chosen at random. Any adult within the selected city block, or rural segment, then becomes a potential respondent. To designate specific persons would be slightly more accurate, but prohibitively expensive.

The panel technique is used to measure changes in opinion. A sample is selected by one of the standard methods, and questions are asked. Six months or a year later, the same persons are rounded up by the interviewers and asked the same questions again—or perhaps slightly different questions. How have group attitudes shifted over the period? The famous Elmira political study, which we will examine in Chapter 7, was a panel operation.

Margins of error for all methods are readily calculable, depending on the size of the sample. The size for a universe of all adult Americans varies between 1,500 and 5,000 respondents. They can give an opinion which dependably approximates that of 100 million. Here is the reason, incidentally, why you may never have been polled in a national survey. In any given poll you have only one chance in 20,000.

Back in the late 1930's, a research agency asked a sample of 30,000 persons whether they favored the revival of the National Recovery Act, the famous NRA.[2] The first 500 replies yielded a "No" vote of 54.9 percent. The final count of 30,000 persons yielded a "No" of 55.5 percent, a difference of six-tenths of a percentage point. The poll taker could have saved a lot of interviewing. Below a certain minimum number of interviews the analyst can get into serious trouble, and above a certain maximum he will waste the client's money.

STEP 4. PHRASING THE QUESTION

At this point good semantic judgment becomes crucial. An issue can be scrambled or even put into reverse by inept wording. In 1940, a poll taker asked: "Do you think the U.S. should do everything in its power to help England and France in their war against Hitler?" The "Yes" vote was overwhelming. Then he asked an equivalent sample: "Do you think the U.S. should become involved in a plan to help England and France in their war against Hitler?" The "Yes" vote dropped sharply. "Involved" is a loaded word; George Washington warned us more than a century and a half ago against foreign entanglements and involvements.

In phrasing the question, only one thing should be asked at a time. "Do you think it wise to put money into real estate and securities?" is bad wording. One respondent may be shy of securities and favor real estate; another the reverse. Always make two separate questions.

In Step 4, we have to decide whether to use "closed" questions, "open" questions, or a combination of both. In closed questions, the respondent has only certain prescribed choices: such as "Yes," "No," "Don't Know." (There can, however, be more than three alternatives.)

In open or open-end questions, the interviewer often begins with a big general question, and then does some probing in depth. For instance, he asks: "What do you think will happen to prices in the next six months?" "Why do you think so?" "What are you doing about your own buying?" And so on. Depth interviewing can be revealing, but the results may be difficult to tabulate. Generally speaking, an open question allows the respondent to give his own answer freely.

Cafeteria questions, described earlier, also must be considered in Step 4.

STEP 5. THE TEST RUN

After the question is worded to the researcher's satisfaction, the next step is to put it up in a trial balloon—take a sample of a sample. In one study which I personally followed closely, 22 questions were tried out on a preliminary group of 100 people. As a result, certain cloudy terms and implications were eliminated before the regular interviewers went on the road to get answers from a nation-wide sample.

STEP 6. THE INTERVIEW

Untrained interviewers can wreck the most careful work on the preceding five steps. It is easier to train an interviewer for closed questions than for open, but good judgment is always required. Most interviewers are intelligent women, working part time, and they are chosen and trained with care. As many as 300 may serve one research agency in a nation-wide survey. The group will speak personally to at least 1,500 respondents, sometimes 5,000, visiting them usually in their homes. For a pure random sample the interviewer must seek out the specific individual whom chance has selected, and come back and come back until the person is found. The same must be done for a panel survey, but not for a quota survey. For a modified random sample the interviewer only needs to find some person in the block, as noted earlier.

In an unemployment survey, interviewers should never ask, "You're not working now, are you?" but rather, "Are you looking for a job now, or waiting for a while?" This approach protects the respondent's pride. Answers must not be put in the respondent's mouth. "Do you say that because of the high cost of living?" will cause many to follow the leader with, "Sure, that's why." A suggestion has been offered and bias is in. All this is worked out in advance by pretesting. The interviewer only reports answers to the tested questions.

There are at least four possible difficulties in the communication line between interviewer and respondent:

1. Deliberate misstatements by respondent for various reasons.

2. Pretense, to bolster the respondent's ego. If the interviewer asks: "What do you think of Zen Buddhism?" she will probably get 95 percent D.K.'s (Don't Knows), while the remaining five percent don't know either, but are pretending they do.

3. Honest mistakes by respondent—thinking he knows where Quemoy is when he really does not know.

4. Attempts by respondent to influence poll results, if he feels a personal interest in the outcome.

I was recently interviewed as a sample item on the question of American investments in the Near East. I try to keep up with many economic developments but not with this one. I was tempted to tell the pleasant, gray-haired lady, with pencil poised, somewhat more than I really knew about investments in Iraq. I resisted the temptation, and probably went on the record as a Don't Know.

Roper reports that accuracy is improved by having Negro interviewers interview Negroes in the South and, where possible, in the North.

STEP 7. TABULATING RESULTS

After the interviewers have made the rounds, their free-hand questionnaires are sent to the central office for coding and tabulating. Results are punched on cards and the cards run through machines which total them and calculate percentages. High-powered mathematics is normally avoided, and the data kept as simple as possible. For interviews in depth, statistics must be used with especial caution. Subjective feelings do not readily lend themselves to punch cards.

STEP 8. REPORTING THE FINAL RESULTS

The director of the survey now takes the figures, discusses them with his staff, and proceeds to write the report for the press, for his own newsletter, or for his client.

An advertising client, for instance, may receive a market survey on the popular response to his new radio set. Gallup conducts a syndicated column for newspapers. Roper's *Public Pulse* goes to a selected list of students of public opinion. Government figures on unemployment go to the head of the department and then out to the press. Rating figures on the popularity of TV programs go to the broadcasters and their anxious sponsors; they can make or break an expensive show. Many, perhaps most, opinion survey reports are never made public.

The report should explain not only what the figures show, but what they do *not* show. The common impulse to generalize from inadequate data must be rigorously suppressed. The director should caution the reader against applying results to a different universe from the one being measured—for instance, against applying the reactions of Kansas farmers to *all* United States farmers. And he must never forget to report the "D.K.'s," and explain them clearly.

CAVEATS

In the early days of opinion research based on sampling theory, skepticism was widespread, especially among political observers who prided themselves on their intuition. The miscalculation of the 1948 presidential campaign strengthened this skepticism. Today, however, practically everybody accepts some sampling results, even if they do not accept many conclusions.

The battle is won so far as the principle is concerned; careful sampling can reflect a given universe within a calculated error of two to five percent.* Large objections, however, are still raised concerning the competence of the question asked, and the care with which technical methods are employed. In summary, the principal objections are these:

If the respondent has little or no experience with the question, or information about it, he can be pushed by an adroit interviewer, or a badly worded question, into almost any answer. Or he may sometimes fabricate an answer to protect his pride.

If the question is concerned with the standard belief system of the culture, most respondents can be expected to give an answer which accords with the proper thing to do, even if they do not do it. A college student in a survey on religious beliefs remarked candidly: "You do things because you want to be seen doing them."

If the question has an answer which most of us know as a matter of common sense, putting it through the elaborate polling process is a ridiculous waste of time and money. "Do you believe in education?" "Do you favor our form of government?" are such silly questions.

A constant danger lies in overgeneralizing the result of a survey, both in space and in time. Polls showed heavy majorities against going to war with the Axis powers in 1940. After the attack on Pearl Harbor, the percentage dropped close to zero. It would thus be utterly wrong to

---

* With this margin of error it is rather silly to show percentages running to decimal points. As one expert puts it: "We simply are not as accurate as the decimal point would indicate." He would also like to have all reports show the size of the sample, and the probable margin of error. I agree with him.

generalize that opinion research proves Americans always for peace. That they have generally been for peace with certain exceptions is the most one can say.

Again, it is wrong to generalize the opinions of a small group of workers as applicable to all workers, or the opinions of all Americans to the people of other countries. Not long after the war, an American poll indicated that 60 percent of Americans believed that "you can trust people," while a German poll showed only six percent who felt that way. Probably the German figure today, with a return to prosperity and self-respect, would be considerably higher—thus bringing in the time factor on top of the space factor.

When a respondent has enough knowledge and experience to give an honest personal opinion on a carefully worded question, free of built-in bias, and uncomplicated by the mores, then we have something which can be of great value to public policy, to public leadership, and to the scientific knowledge of human behavior. I have tried to keep this standard in mind in the chapters to come, but it is improbable that I have always been successful.

NO TURNING BACK

Hadley Cantril has observed that bias is ever lurking in the background in opinion research, but, he says, "a tool must be evaluated not against an absolute standard of efficiency but against the efficiency of alternative tools that are available." The chief alternatives now available are hunch, guess, finger-in-the-wind judgments, and personal predilections.

After some 20 years of experimenting by reputable analysts, Hyman and Sheatsley summarized the findings in a scholarly study, as cited earlier.[1] Of the vast body of data collected up to 1950, the authors concluded that much was ephemeral, but that certain permanent or hard profiles of American opinion had emerged. It was possible to discern, they said, within fluctuating votes on particular issues, some of the basic beliefs and judgments of the American people. Interpretation may be disputed, but it can be regarded as certain "that if the entire U.S. population had been confronted by the same question at the same time, the results would not have varied by more than a few percentage points."

William A. Lydgate has expressed a similar conclusion: "No longer does the American mass mind represent a trackless, uncharted sea to be glimpsed only by guesswork, inference and intuition, by some flash of insight by a Bryce, a Dana, a Greeley or a Lippmann. . . ."[3]

There are two cross tests, in addition to the test of comparing political polls with election results. First, if a carefully worded question receives a high percentage of agreement, or disagreement, year after year, validity can be assumed high. Again, if two independent polling agencies, using different brigades of interviewers at a similar time, come up with close agreement in the answer to a carefully worded, identical question, obviously we have an opinion we can rely on.

Interviewers ringing doorbells find many respondents weighed down with the burden of personal problems—women worn out with the daily care of large families, with poverty and illness. It is remarkable, observe Hyman and Sheatsley, that they respond as intelligently as they do. More education is not the only remedy. "Sometimes the task is only to free people from their pressing concern with personal problems so that they may have opportunity to look out to broader horizons." It may well be, as living standards rise in an affluent society, that public attitudes will grow more firm and dependable.

Many answers in the pages to come will show alarming ignorance, while many will show a surprising amount of information, and a high quality of judgment. This is as perplexing as it is instructive. We need the reliable results of scientific sampling.*

Let Samuel Stouffer sum it up. Opinion research, he said, can replace myths with realities. "We, as social scientists, have an obligation to make the tools better and better, and we, as citizens, have an obligation to see that these powerful instruments are wisely employed. There is no turning back."

* A frank and illuminating discussion of the technical aspects of polling is found in a pamphlet published by the Center for the Study of Democratic Institutions in Santa Barbara in 1962. Donald McDonald interviews Roper and Gallup on their difficulties and successes.

3
FOREIGN POLICY

What is the attitude of Americans toward the world outside, as shown by the polls? What foreign policies do they want the United States to pursue? How far are citizens aware of the imperatives of the nuclear age?

In this field of crisis after crisis, where experts disagree, and the press is often partisan, public opinion frequently becomes a critical factor. How far can a President go, toward war or peace, without encountering mass resistance? In the analysis to follow, we shall find a good deal of ignorance and confusion; nevertheless, certain trends appear with significant consistency. First let us consider some over-all reactions.

THE DECLINE OF ISOLATIONISM

"What do you think is the most important problem facing the country today?" *

The Gallup News Service asked this question four times

---

* I have sometimes shortened the poll questions quoted in this study.

within three years, using a nation-wide sample, based on the modified random sample method.[1] In March, 1961, results were as follows:

Keeping the peace	55%
Unemployment	25
High cost of living	11
Racial integration	6
D.K. (Don't Know)	3
	100

Earlier, in October, 1960, peace ranked even higher, unemployment lower but still in second place.

In September, 1959, results were scattered: [2]

Keeping the peace, dealing with Russia	51 %
Maintaining economic balance	14
Integration of the races	5
Unemployment	4
Juvenile delinquency	4
Danger of atomic testing	3
Strikes	3
All others	13
D.K.	8
Total	105 *

Still earlier, in 1958, the same question—"What do you think is the most important problem"—showed "Keeping the peace" and affiliated problems at close to 50 percent,

* Some respondents gave more than one item as "most important."

followed by unemployment, racial integration, and the
high cost of living, each in the neighborhood of 10 percent.[3]

That United States foreign policy is a long-term anxiety
is confirmed by a much earlier *Fortune* poll, published in
July, 1948. Respondents were asked whether the President
to be elected should be primarily skilled in national or
international affairs. Half of all voted for skill in international affairs, less than a third for skill in domestic affairs. The rest didn't know.

Again, polling a nation-wide sample of adults just before the 1960 presidential election, Roper found foreign
affairs worrying citizens far more than domestic affairs.[4]
Relations with Russia led the foreign list (this was after
the U-2 incident), racial integration led the list of domestic worries.

The Japanese attack on Pearl Harbor in 1941 was a
turning point in American public opinion. Up to that date,
all careful polls showed majorities against going to war.
As the outrages of Hitler increased, percentages declined
but never fell below 50 percent. Ever since that "day of
infamy" most Americans have felt themselves seriously
involved in international affairs, and with a military responsibility—thus reversing a century and more of isola-
tion.

In 1953, 81 percent of respondents in a poll reported
by Roper said it would be impossible to stay out of a big
war in Europe; 60 percent said the same for Asia.

FOREIGN AID

"Do you think it is a good policy for the U.S. to help backward countries raise their standard of living, or shouldn't this be any concern of our government?" [5] Seventy-three percent of Americans thought it a good policy in 1952, when the question was asked by University of Chicago researchers. Twenty-three percent thought it no concern of our government; four percent didn't know. Of those who believed foreign aid a sound policy, almost half thought the money should be handled in whole or in part by the United Nations.

In 1958, Gallup asked, "How do you feel about foreign aid?" with this result: [6]

For it	51%
Against it	32
D.K. and no answer	17
	100

PEACE CORPS

There can be little doubt about the popularity of President Kennedy's Peace Corps, another large international venture. In early 1961, a poll showed 71 percent of respondents in favor of it, only 18 percent opposed.[7] Eleven percent had not made up their minds. When the question "Would you like to have your son participate?" was asked, two-thirds of respondents said "Yes," a quarter said "No." The opposition was mostly associated with two slogans: "Down with foreigners," and "Too much spending already."

The American Council on Education sent letters to 950 college presidents asking their opinion of the Peace Corps. Those who replied were in favor of it nine to one. This is, of course, a highly selected universe, but a proper one, I think, for a question connected with education.

ATTITUDES TOWARD NUCLEAR WAR

Thermonuclear warfare, scientists agree, is different not only in degree but in kind, compared to all wars of the past. It introduces two elements hitherto unknown, as well as an incredible increase in blast, heat and firestorm. First, the chief victims of World War III are likely to be civilians, rather than members of the armed forces. Secondly, nuclear war will release lethal radioactivity which may descend for years over the entire planet. Biologists predict that this will poison the pool of genes on which the future of the race depends.

How do Americans feel about this grim prospect? Roper reported in 1952 that 82 percent of a national cross section feared terrible destruction in the event of nuclear war. Only nine percent said "not much." Thus awareness of what atomic scientists call "doomsday" has been high in the public mind for a long time. The book and the motion picture *On the Beach* have undoubtedly played a part, though efforts have been made to modify anxiety, through such books as that of Herman Kahn on thermonuclear war.

Here is more evidence of awareness. A poll in 1958 found a majority of respondents believing that seven out of 10 Americans would not live through a thermonuclear attack.[8] "The U.S. people," said Gallup, "are in great awe of the death-dealing potential of the hydrogen bomb."

A Gilbert Youth Survey in 1959 showed 90 percent of U.S. teen-agers fearing that nuclear war would eventually destroy the race.

A California questionnaire poll in 1960 asked 2,000 people in San Francisco and 1,000 in Sonoma County: "Do you believe the avoidance of nuclear war is the most important issue before the U.S. today?" [9] "Yes," said about three-quarters of the city dwellers and two-thirds of the rural people.

Surveys made by the Atomic Energy Commission in 1958 throw an interesting light on the whole question. Americans may fear nuclear war, but in that year only 12 percent of them could define fall-out in broad general terms, let alone in technical detail. About a third had never heard of radioactive fall-out. It is reasonable to suppose that since the Berlin crisis of 1961, knowledge has increased. Most shelters are recommended specifically for fall-out, not for blast and burn.

PARADOX

Yet with all this mental recognition of danger, the reaction to it has been comparatively mild. In a nation-wide survey conducted by Gallup for the *Saturday Evening Post,* published in late December, 1961, two-thirds of all young people expected nuclear war in their time, but only 14 percent said it was their greatest fear.

Various explanations have been offered; and here is one from opinion research, which shows a curious paradox.[10]

"Statements and warnings of danger are likely to be less effective as the threat becomes more *extreme.* An audience whose anxieties have been too highly stimulated apparently tends to recoil, rather than learn, or to consider."

A classic example was found in a study of high school students. Three groups of students were shown three different film versions of the danger of dental neglect, and all were urged to see a dentist. Thirty-six percent of those who viewed the minimum threat went to the dentist, 22 percent of those who viewed the middle threat went, but only eight percent of those exposed to the *maximum* threat went to the dentist. "Differences between the groups were still apparent a full year later."

How natural for normal people, who may fear to face a dentist, to refuse to face—or even think through—the threat of nuclear war. It involves imagining the details of one's own death, which psychologists say is difficult if not impossible for a healthy individual.

SHELTERS AND CIVIL DEFENSE

A study in 1952 concluded that emphasis on the horrors of nuclear bombing was a "peculiarly ineffective way to stimulate civilian defense." [10] Few Americans took any steps to protect themselves from nuclear attack before the fall of 1961. A poll in 1960 found that 89 percent of respondents had done nothing.[11] Seventy-one percent at that time favored a law requiring the construction of *public* bomb shelters, 19 percent were opposed to such a law, 10 percent didn't know. In the same poll, 79 percent said they had given no thought to building a home shelter.

This 1960 survey concluded: "Only one family in nine has taken any steps to prepare for all-out nuclear war."

A year later, in August, 1961, Gallup found that nearly a quarter of all families said they had made some preparation, most of them by storing food.[12]

The *New York Times,* in the fall of 1961, took a sidewalk poll of more than 100 New Yorkers, from which the *Times* concluded that people in and near large cities "feel that protection against a superbomb at this time is almost hopeless." [13] Most respondents were apartment dwellers, and none had built shelters. "Almost all believed that the government had failed them by not building or subsidizing public and private shelters." Many had no idea what to do if a superbomb fell on New York, and expressed some guilt that they had not bothered to find out. A few felt that instant death was preferable to survival amid the radioactive wreckage. Here are some comments:

An accountant living in Queens: "I've experienced one war and bombings already. But survival with fall-out from these 'dirty' bombs would be miserable. I'd rather be dead, and my wife and children, too."

A Stamford, Connecticut, real estate dealer: "It's all pretty ridiculous. If the bombs really start blowing there will be little that people can do to save themselves. What kind of a world will they find when they emerge from their shelters? Everything will be contaminated, and probably nothing left standing. It would not be the kind of world I'd want to live in."

A bank teller on Second Avenue: "I live in an apartment house. Where could I go? The only thing I could do would be to run to the basement, or run under the bomb and get it over with quickly."

These sidewalk comments are from only a few individuals, living in a metropolitan area which would doubtless be a prime target in World War III. If we take a nation-wide sample, however, on a more scientific basis, the result is not too different. The question was asked in September, 1961: "If we get into a nuclear war what do you think your *own* chances would be of living through it?" [14]

Poor	43%
Fifty-fifty	40
Good	9
D.K.	8
	100

Only one person in 11 thought his chance of survival was good. Respondents in cities with populations of 50,-000 and up were sure they lived in a prime target area. These figures indicate, says Gallup, "the grim reality in American thinking about nuclear war." Even people in small towns were frightened, the sample showed. This reaction differs in personal intensity from all previous polls, and was undoubtedly due to the Berlin crisis of 1961, the resumption of nuclear tests by Russia, and official publicity advising fall-out shelters.

ATTITUDES TOWARD RUSSIA

In both world wars Russia was our ally; today many Americans regard her as a deadly enemy. It is significant

to note how the image of Russia held by the public has
changed. In 1942, a sample of 1,200 citizens was asked to
select from a list of 25 adjectives those which best described the Russian character.[15] Six years later, in 1948,
when the Cold War was getting under way, UNESCO
asked the question again:

Russians are:

	1942	1948	Change
Hard working	61%	49%	Down
Brave	48	28	Down
Progressive	24	15	Down
Practical	18	13	Down
Intelligent	16	12	Down
Cruel	9	50	Way up
Conceited	3	28	Way up

The wartime virtues were downgraded in 1948, the
faults greatly upgraded, as ally changed to enemy. By
contrast, the public image of Germany, a deadly enemy in
1942, has been reversed. Germans were called, in order:[16]

In 1942	In 1961
Warlike	Hard working
Hard working	Intelligent
Cruel	Progressive
Treacherous	Practical
Intelligent	Brave

Using this scale, how do Americans see themselves?
Well, we do not precisely hate ourselves. The five adjec-

tives most frequently used are, in order: peace-loving, generous, intelligent, progressive, brave.[15]

Stouffer asked a nation-wide sample in 1955: "Of these three ways of dealing with Russia, which do you think is best for America now?" [17]

	All adults	Community leaders
Fight Russia	14%	13%
Ignore her	17	17
Negotiate with her	61	62
D.K.	8	8
	100	100

People and leaders were in close agreement, with negotiation favored by large majorities of each.

Roper, in 1953, found only six percent of Americans in favor of a so-called "preventive war"—the military jargon is "preclusive war"—while 59 percent favored negotiation supported by a strong military position, and so stood in close agreement with the Stouffer survey. A majority of respondents thought Russia should remain a member of the United Nations, while a quarter of them disagreed.

Gallup, in 1959, found a majority believing that peace with Russia was possible sooner or later.[18] In June, 1960, however, after the U-2 incident and the breakup of the Summit Conference in Paris, the vote was reversed; a majority expected war with Russia some day.

Late in 1960 the figures were reversed again, as this question was asked: "Do you believe that it is possible to reach a peaceful settlement with Russia?" [19]

	All adults	College education	High school education	Grade school only
It is possible	50%	61%	51%	42%
It is not	27	23	30	26
D.K.	23	16	19	32
	100	100	100	100

Fear, generated by collapse at the Summit, abated toward the end of 1960. Note, however, the large percentage of uncertainty, with a third of grade schoolers registering "Don't Know."

In June, 1961, a nation-wide sample was asked: "Who's ahead in the missile race?" [20] A majority said the United States was ahead—a natural patriotic reaction. I am afraid, however, that this is an example of a useless question. The public has almost no knowledge of the technology of missiles, and the various aspects which may be competitive. The evaluation of "who's ahead" is a complex matter shrouded in military secrecy.

In May, 1961, Gallup asked a more meaningful question in the same general area: "It has been estimated that it would cost the U.S. $40 billions to send a man to the moon. Would you like to see that amount spent for this purpose or not?" [21]

"No," said a working majority of 58 percent; "Yes," said 33 percent. We laymen may know little about the technology of flights through space, but we appear to know something about relative costs.

BERLIN CRISIS

The crisis over Berlin which has kept recurring ever since the air lift in 1948, reached a climax with the building of the wall between East and West Berlin in August, 1961.

In November, 1961, Gallup asked: "If Communist East Germany closes all roads to Berlin and does not permit planes to land in Berlin, do you think the U.S. and its allies should, or should not, try to fight their way into Berlin?" [22]

	U.S.	Gallup poll in Canada
We should fight our way in	62%	47%
We should not	20	33
D.K.	18	20
	100	100

Americans were more belligerent than Canadians, but both were more ready to fight than not. Observe, however, that the fight was to be conducted jointly with our allies, and directed against East Germany. Russia was not mentioned in this question. A similar reason for fighting was given by many respondents in both Canada and the United States: "We must stand firm somewhere, or the Communists will take over all Europe."

Russia comes into the next question in this same survey: "If Russia insists on controlling Berlin, do you think this will lead to a fighting war or not?" [22]

	U.S.	Canada
Yes, it will lead to war	59%	61%
No, it will not	27	27
D.K.	14	12
	100	100

Gallup does not ask whether we *should* fight, but whether the action will lead to a fight, and six out of 10 citizens in both countries believe that it will.

What kind of a war do we expect over Berlin? A nation-wide poll taken in July, 1961, found 59 percent of us worried that it might be a nuclear war.[23] Women were more worried than men. Another survey in the same month showed four out of 10 Americans believing that a war which began with conventional weapons would escalate to nuclear weapons.[24] A majority thought not—perhaps because they hoped not.

The question has not been asked, so far as I know, whether the United States would use nuclear weapons if our troops were being driven out of Germany by superior Russian ground and air forces. Presumably a majority again would answer "Yes." The public has been uneasily aware that war with Russia would be a nuclear war sooner or later.

What do the people of West Berlin think about it? A poll taken in November, 1961, shows that 49 percent of West Berliners believed war unlikely, 36 percent believed there is some possibility, and only five percent believed that war is "very likely." [25] The Berliners were not nearly so pessimistic as, say, New Yorkers. But here we have to make allowances. Anybody living in Berlin in the fall of 1961, would, if he were human, strongly desire to escape incineration.

What do the French think about it? A poll in November, 1961, asked people whether Berlin was worth a war.[26] "No," said 70 percent. "Few Frenchmen seem to care at all about what happens to Germans."

"Do you think the U.N. should try to settle the Berlin problem?" [27] Gallup asked this in July, 1961, of a nationwide U.S. sample. "Yes," said 81 percent. "*Can* the U.N. settle it?" "Yes," said 40 percent; "No," said 40 percent; 20 percent had no answer. The U.N., Americans thought, should try, but success was problematical. Again, the pessimism, the uneasiness, but no vigorous response.

CUBA

Cuba is as much a problem in United States relations with Russia as in our relations with Latin America. This fact undoubtedly influences answers to questions about Cuba, but it is impossible to measure to what extent.

"What should be our policy in Cuba?" The question was asked soon after the April, 1961, fiasco in Pigs Bay, with these results: [28]

	Send in the Marines	Aid anti-Castro forces	Stop trading with Cuba
Yes	24%	44%	63%
No	65	41	23
D.K.	11	15	14
	100	100	100

Thus two-thirds of respondents were against military intervention even after a severe blow to American prestige. Intervention would be favored, Gallup reported, only if Russia attempted to establish a military base in Cuba.

Seventy percent of us thought that we should work with other Latin American countries and with the U.N. on the Cuban problem. Only 15 percent were in favor of going it alone. Curiously enough, after President Kennedy assumed blame for the disastrous landing by anti-Castro forces, his popularity index rose to an all-time high; 83 percent of us thought he was "doing a good job." This was higher than any figure achieved by Eisenhower in eight years of the Presidency. Why? It would take a lot of depth interviewing to find out.

CHINA

Opposition by Americans to admitting Red China into the United Nations has been massive over the years, as the following figures show. "Do you think Communist China should or should not be admitted as a member of the U.N.?" [29] The "No" vote was:

In 1950	58%	1957	70%
1954	79	1958	66
1955	67	1961 (March)	64
1956	74	1961 (October)	65

Close to two-thirds of Americans are now in 1962 against admission. But the accent shifts when people are asked: "If a majority of the U.N. decided to admit Com-

munist China, should the U.S. go along?" "Yes," said 46
percent in October, 1961; "No," said 38 percent; D.K., 16
percent. Polls show only a minority of respondents expecting Chiang ever to return to the mainland.

Comparisons with Britain and Canada on the subject
of admitting Red China are interesting. In 1961, 64 percent of Americans opposed it, but only 39 percent of
Canadians, with 50 percent in favor.[30] Only 28 percent of
Britons were opposed, with 43 percent in favor of admission. The British D.K. vote, however, was large, 29 percent.

When the China crisis was at its height in 1958, and
the offshore islands under terrible bombardment from the
mainland, only half of us could name Quemoy as a principal trouble spot; only 30 percent could name Matsu. A
Roper poll came up with these significant figures: [31]

Ready to fight for Quemoy and Formosa	16%
Ready to fight for Formosa only	20
Total ready to fight	36
Not ready to fight for either	47
D.K.	17
	100

Americans are gradually coming to realize the importance of mainland China, even if opposition to formal recognition remains large. A poll in 1961 showed half of us
believing that the United States should try to "improve
relations" with Red China.[32] A poll of leading citizens,
taken by the Council on Foreign Relations in 29 American

communities in 1961, showed that 45 percent of respondents in some degree favored seating Red China in the U.N., while 50 percent were unfavorably inclined. Five percent were undecided.[33]

So far as I know, unlike the situation in Russia, no public opinion polls have ever been set up in Red China. They would make interesting reading, rigged or unrigged.

In the next chapter, we will continue an examination of attitudes toward foreign policy, but with the accent on constructive suggestions for a world without war.

4

TOWARD ONE WORLD

Americans want a world without war, although they are
none too sure it is possible. In the nation-wide survey
made by the Gallup organization for *Look,* published in
early 1960, a quarter of respondents expected a world war
within five years; almost half expected one sooner or later.[1]
"We've always had wars and always will," was a recurring
comment. Most of us assumed that nuclear weapons would
be used. "Yet," said *Look,* "it seems clear that a great
many people cannot visualize what nuclear warfare would
mean." Some mothers were more worried about a son going overseas than about the home town being wiped out
in one blinding flash. "We're pretty far removed from
outer space out here on Seventy-first Street."

When citizens were asked if they expected another
world war within five years, a significant difference due to
education appeared in the "Yes" vote.

Grade school only	29%	"Yes"
High school	22	
College	17	

The more years in school the less the expectation of war. There are several possible explanations for this interesting correlation. One could be the intensity of the individual's desire for peace. Some educated people, the report notes, feel the obligation to express their desire in action of some kind. Nevertheless, those who feel a personal responsibility for world peace do not know what to do about it. A salesman in New Mexico gave a typical answer to an interviewer for the *Look* story: "I suppose we could do more if we paid more attention, but who has the time? We have our own problems."

The study back in 1948 reported by Hadley Cantril compared the outlook for peace in five nations, asking: "Do you think there will be another big war in the next 10 years?" [2]

	Yes	No	D.K.
United States sample	57%	26%	17%
Italy	58	26	16
Norway	53	27	20
Netherlands	52	34	14
England	35	36	29

All but England showed a majority of respondents expecting war. Ten years have come and gone since 1948, and the British came nearest to guessing correctly.

Cantril reports a close finish in the late 1940's. Forty-nine percent of a U.S. sample felt that world peace was possible, while 45 percent thought it impossible. Polls in Britain, France, and West Germany at this time indicated that a majority of citizens believed peace was possible; but majorities did *not* think so in Australia, Italy, Mexico, the Netherlands, and Norway. Mexico was the most dubious, and also had the highest illiteracy rate of any of the countries polled.

Peace in the early years of the nuclear age seemed to resemble the timid sprite in the familiar cartoons. Recent crises in Laos, Algeria, the Congo, Cuba, and especially Berlin, have not made her any bolder.

Gallup surveys show that the fear of world war within five years declined from a high of 58 percent in 1951, to 18 percent in 1959, when President Eisenhower entertained Mr. Khrushchev at Camp David.[3] The Berlin crisis, however, raised the rate of fear to 53 percent in October, 1961.

THE UNITED NATIONS

What have we to offset these fears? What hopes do people cherish about the future? Wendell Willkie once wrote a book, based on a trip around the globe, in which he said very forcibly that we were all members of one world. He wrote it five years before the nuclear age began at Hiroshima. How do Americans respond to such ideas? Their response to the United Nations makes a good starting point for the investigation.

The Carnegie Endowment for World Peace has summarized more than 100 polls dealing with the United Na-

tions, conducted during the 10 years 1945 through 1954.[4]
About 80 percent of respondents in poll after poll voted
to keep the United States in the U.N. The pull-out vote
never exceeded 13 percent—despite the spirited manifes-
tos of the Daughters of the American Revolution in convention assembled. Even if Red China were admitted,
majorities favored staying in the U.N.

The United Nations was seen by most respondents, said
the Carnegie report, as an organization which could help
to prevent a war; but only a minority saw it as a means
for administering a warless world. Popular information
about the United Nations was meager; about one-fifth of
Americans during these 10 years had a very hazy picture
of its operations.

In times of crisis, satisfaction with U.N. performance
tended to decline; in less hectic times satisfaction increased. During the fighting in Korea, opinion fluctuated
with the fortunes of war. The Inchon landing by General
MacArthur in 1950 produced the highest satisfaction index
during the whole 10-year period—65 percent of respondents thought the U.N. was doing a good job. When the
Red Chinese crossed the Yalu River, the index of satisfaction dropped sharply to 30 percent.

The Carnegie study found that support of the United
Nations as a principle was very different from support
based on its performance. The well-informed had more
confidence in it than the ill-informed, but wanted to
strengthen its structure so that it might perform better.
The more a respondent knew about the United Nations,
the more moderate his satisfaction with its performance.

He was more realistic, less subject to hopes and fears, than the ill-informed respondent.

Two kinds of people opposed the U.N. during the 10-year period: surviving isolationists, and all-out supporters of a World State. The latter paradox probably arose because the World Staters considered the U.N. too ineffective to be worth saving. But the combined opposition, as noted earlier, never went above 13 percent.

These reactions to the United Nations showed no significant difference between regions in the United States, none based on sex, age, or political party affiliation. Once more, however, they showed a marked correlation with education. The more years in school, the more likely a respondent was:

To be informed about the U.N.
To regard it as important for world peace.
To advocate continued U.S. membership and interest, especially by Congress.
To favor a stronger structure.
To be dissatisfied with current performance.

The Carnegie report concludes that the findings up to 1955 may or may not be valid today, but present a working hypothesis. Other surveys bear out this hypothesis. Said Elmo Roper in a 1953 broadcast:

The people of this country are behind the United Nations. Wherever the question is asked, opinion surveys show that seven out of ten people—in round numbers about 75 million people—think the United States is better off because of the United Nations. . . .

People are concerned that if we scrapped the U.N., we might scrap the last best hope for peace.

The United Nations is definitely something for Americans to cling to in these years of crisis. In early 1961 Gallup asked: "How important do you think it is that we try to make the United Nations a success?" [5] Very important, said 83 percent; fairly important, said another eight percent—bringing the total to nine out of 10 Americans. Gallup also reports that for several years before the U.N. was organized in 1945, the public had favored the creation of such an international organization, and it has strongly supported the U.N. ever since.

How about tangible performance? Samples from four nations in 1961 replied as follows to the question: "Do you think the United Nations is doing a good job?" [6]

	U.S.	Britain	West Germany	France
Fair to good	79%	70%	63%	39%
Poor	11	16	9	33
D.K.	10	14	28	28
	100	100	100	100

The United States was far and away the most satisfied, with the lowest D.K. vote as well. The people of France were the least satisfied. High approval of the U.N. was reported at the same time in Ireland, the Netherlands, Denmark, Switzerland, and Finland, all ranging around 60 percent.

In crisis after crisis Americans have advocated action by the United Nations.[7] A majority wanted the U.N. to handle aid to Greece in 1947. Eighty percent were behind U.N. action in Korea. Seventy percent favored sending a U.N. police force to maintain order in the Gaza strip in Israel after the war with Egypt. Ninety-one percent of us, familiar with the situation, wished the U.N. to settle the Quemoy and Matsu crisis in 1958. Three out of four in 1960 favored a U.N. police force in the Congo.[8]

So much for the reaction of a universe composed of all adult Americans. Let us now restrict the universe to Americans of note. The Bureau of Applied Research at Columbia University in 1960 queried a random sample * of 1,294 persons listed in Who's Who in America.[7] The following figures indicate not only a high level of support for the U.N., but considerable thought about machinery for enforcing world peace:

76 percent, three quarters of Who's Who, favored giving U.N. courts the power to settle disputes between nations.

68 percent, two-thirds, said the U.N. should have a police force to enforce court decisions.

66 percent said the United States should take the lead in making specific proposals to establish a system of enforceable world law.

59 percent thought that U.N. membership should be open to all nations (presumably including China and Germany).

* This would be a "file" sample.

68 percent were in favor of abolishing the veto in the Security Council of the U.N.

UNIVERSE OF LAWYERS

In a more specific inquiry, a questionnaire was sent in 1959 to members of the American Bar Association, including all members of the House of Delegates and presidents of state and local bar associations, and a random sample of junior members.[9] Replies were received from 297 lawyers with this result:

1. A majority favored world peace through world law, and felt that the goal was not beyond reasonable hope.

2. A majority favored a broader use of the present World Court, and believed that the Court, not the United States, should decide whether a given dispute was within the Court's jurisdiction. The "Connally Amendment," now on the books, gives the United States government the power to decide what questions are internal. These lawyers favored rescinding the Amendment.

3. A majority thought a presidential commission should be created to make specific recommendations for promoting world peace through world law.

The above is, I believe, a legitimate use of a universe restricted to technical experts, and of the questionnaire method. It is doubtful if the general public understands the Connally Amendment well enough to express a useful opinion.

CONGRESSMAN'S UNIVERSE

Here is another questionnaire poll. It undoubtedly contains some elements of bias, but is nevertheless significant. In 1961, William B. Widnall, Republican Congressman from New Jersey, mailed 60,000 questionnaires to his constituents.[10] He received 12,000 replies—doubtless from the more literate and the more interested—with this result:

84 percent thought the United Nations the best hope to maintain world peace.

72 percent said that complete general disarmament should be one of the primary objectives of U.S. foreign policy.

77 percent favored a world rule of law, backed by a World Court and enforced by an international armed force.

81 percent thought that the U.N. should be strengthened.

73 percent said that the United States should take the lead in furthering the above measures—in spite of the current uncooperative attitude of the Soviet Union.

It is interesting to note that the members of *Who's Who in America,* of the American Bar Association, and of Congressman Widnall's district, all agree that the United States should take the lead in formal proposals for a world rule of law.

Another expression of internationalism is support for a world auxiliary language. Gallup, in 1953, asked adults in the United States, Canada, the Netherlands, Norway, and Finland if school children should be taught an international language. Large majorities in all countries voted "Yes." (The children did not vote.)

TEST BAN

In 1958, when the United States was still testing nuclear weapons, Roper asked a nation-wide sample about banning such tests: [11]

Stop testing whether Russia does or not	9%
Agree with Russia to stop testing, without an inspection system	12
Agree with Russia, with a system of inspection	37
Total favoring test ban in some form	58
Continue testing whatever Russia does	31
D.K.	11
	100

Most of those in favor of the test ban wanted inspection included. The nine percent who voted for the ban on a unilateral basis may or may not have represented the percentage of Americans in favor of unilateral disarmament.

Gallup, in December, 1959, after both the United States and Russia had voluntarily stopped testing, asked people if they wanted the ban to continue. "Yes," said 77 percent; "No," said 11 percent. Americans thus approved the voluntary ban by a vote of seven to one. This vote came, be it observed, after the ban had been tried. Before the trial, as the Roper poll above shows, only 58 percent were in favor.

Soon after Russia broke the voluntary ban in the fall of 1961, Gallup asked samples in three countries: "What do you think the United States should do now—start tests again, or continue the ban on H-bomb tests?"[12]

	U.S.*	Britain	India **
U.S. should start testing	59%	30%	18%
Should not	30	64	69
D.K.	11	6	13
	100	100	100

U.S. city dwellers voted two to one in favor of a resumption of testing, while people in Britain voted two to one against it, and Indians four to one against. Distance seemed to lend disenchantment.

The United States government followed the wish of city dwellers and resumed testing, with the explanation that these were to be underground tests, with no danger of fall-out. There could, of course, be some danger to underground waters. When citizens were asked in 1961 if we should emulate Russia by testing in the atmosphere, 44 percent said "Yes"; 45 percent said "No"; 11 percent didn't know.[13] The fear of fall-out was chiefly behind the "No" vote, but Gallup also reported some fear of continuing the arms race.

"If we start testing now," said a New York City house-

* Respondents in New York City, Chicago, Los Angeles, only.
** Respondents in New Delhi only.

wife, "it will create forces that could bring about war and destruction. If we start, the Russians will do more of it, and there'll be no end." A Fall River policeman voiced the opposite position: "If we don't start testing, Russia will get too far ahead." The fact that each country possesses a stock pile ample to destroy the other several times over did not seem to register with most respondents.

DISARMAMENT

Public sentiment for disarmament is far greater now than before Americans became aware of the nuclear age. We mostly favor it, but with fluctuating majorities, depending on the news. A survey in early 1946 showed two to one *against* a proposal that Russia, Britain, and the United States get together to abolish armaments and military training.[14] This was only a few months after Hiroshima.

By the summer of 1955, however, two-thirds of us favored disarmament, *if all major nations disarmed.* In July, 1958, 70 percent supported a world organization which would guarantee, by careful inspection, that no nation produced nuclear weapons.

In the fall of 1959, when Khrushchev, speaking at the United Nations, proposed complete disarmament in four years, but with no plan for inspection, 60 percent of us thought the proposal a propaganda stunt. Only 20 percent believed him sincere.

In November, 1960, Gallup addressed the following question to a nation-wide sample: "If Russia agrees to disarm under careful inspection by the U.N., should the U.S. agree to disarm to the same extent?" [14]

	All citizens	College graduates
Yes	46%	60%
No	41	36
D.K.	13	4
	100	100

Disarmament was still favored under these conditions but not by much, except among college graduates, who showed a substantial majority in favor.

A year later, in November, 1961, Gallup asked nation-wide samples in both America and Britain if they thought Khrushchev was bluffing in his repeated pleas for disarmament.[15] Seventy-nine percent of Americans and 50 percent of Britons believed him to be bluffing. Only nine percent of Americans and 21 percent of Britons thought him sincere.

SUMMARY NOTE

These chapters on attitudes toward foreign policy and one world demonstrate conclusively that most Americans want a world from which wars are banned, and wish a supranational authority to settle disputes and crises. We feel that this is a more important goal than the solution of any domestic problem, but we are none too confident that such a world is attainable.

The reader will form his own judgment of the results shown in these chapters. To me they seem to indicate an underlying strain of common sense in the majority of Americans. In certain important issues ignorance and confusion are wide-spread, public apathy is often disturbing, percentages shift with the news. Some results seem irrational to me, such as the refusal to admit the existence of Red China. By and large, however, I think the people have done as well as their leaders—and occasionally a good deal better.

5
THE BUSINESS SYSTEM

In this chapter we shall ask Americans what they think of their economic system. Do they want more "socialism," or less? Do they want more social security legislation? What do they think of the "welfare state"? How do they regard Big Business; is more regulation in order? What is their attitude toward installment buying and other forms of consumer debt? Toward savings and the purchase of common stocks? Do they fear inflation? These questions have been answered at various dates by a series of dependable opinion surveys. Sometimes opinion will shift suddenly, but much of it remains fairly constant, or changes slowly over the years.

THE APPEAL OF SOCIALISM

Away back in 1942, half a year after Pearl Harbor, a *Fortune* poll gave an indication of how Americans felt about their economic system at the time.[1] The survey came after two drastic upheavals in economic behavior—

73

the Great Depression of the 1930's which led to the New Deal, and the severe government regulations and disciplines demanded by World War II. A clear plurality of Americans did not want a comprehensive system of "socialism." Forty percent were against it, 25 percent favored it, 35 percent didn't know.

The same poll showed, however, that majorities did want a number of services which come under the head of the "welfare state," including:

Old-age pensions for every one over 65	75% in favor
Medical care for every one who needs it	74
Jobs for the unemployed in public works	68
Unemployment insurance in the interim	58
Increased regulation of the banks	57

A large majority did not want incomes limited by law, though respondents felt that after the war there would be relatively fewer rich people. Large majorities also opposed the regulation of the automobile business and the grocery business.

Twice as many Americans, in this *Fortune* poll, believed that life would be better after the war as believed the contrary. (Was it?) Twice as many believed that a young man would have more opportunity after the war. (Did he?) A plurality believed that the mass unemployment characteristic of the decade of the 1930's would decline after the war. (They were right.)

Fortune thus gives us a kind of base line for majority attitudes toward the economic system. Twenty years ago we were against socialism in the classical sense of "the public ownership of the means of production," but we favored old-age pensions, unemployment insurance, medical care, and other social security provisions.

Another *Fortune* poll, in 1948, showed that the popular feeling against socialism was stronger than in the war years: [2]

	Age 18 to 25	Age 40 to 55
We should maintain our present system	75%	77%
Change to government ownership	18	14
D.K.	7	9
	100	100

The federal government at the time was supporting the popular view by selling most of its huge investment in war plants to private businessmen.

A Gallup survey in 1949 asked a nation-wide sample, after giving the standard definition of socialism: "Would you like to see the United States go more in the direction of socialism or less in the direction of socialism or stay as it is?" [3] Sixty-one percent voted for less; 15 percent for more; and 15 percent for standing pat.

WELFARE LEGISLATION

The public approval of social security and welfare provisions, well marked in 1942, continued after the war. In 1948 *Fortune* asked whether social security should continue to apply to just some people or be extended to cover all people.[4] Eighty-two percent of adult Americans voted to extend the coverage to all; 10 percent were opposed.

Another *Fortune* poll in the same year presented this question: "Do you think we should have laws providing for relief to needy persons?" [5]

Yes, federal laws	40%
Yes, state laws	47
Total affirmative	87
No laws	3
D.K.	10
	100

A survey by Roper in 1952 asked if the law recently passed by Congress, which provided government pensions for all over 65, was a good thing.[6] The affirmative vote was 90 percent. Only two percent believed it a mistake.

Wallace's Farmer ran a questionnaire poll of farmers in February, 1956. "Here are three statements. Which best fits your ideas?"

1. Social security is a wonderful thing	53%
2. It is a good thing on the whole	31
3. It is just another step toward socialism	8
D.K.	8
	100

The above polls bring out a significant difference between abstract and concrete questions. When people were asked if they favored the "welfare state," reaction was consistently negative—thus a survey in 1949: "Does the

idea of the 'welfare state' sound good or poor to you?"
"Poor," said 44 percent; "Fair," said eight percent; "Good,"
said only 28 percent.[3]

But when a sample was asked a few months later if the
government should increase or decrease specific social security measures like medical care, the figures were reversed.[7] Forty-four percent voted for an increase in social
security; only 16 percent for a decrease; while 32 percent
thought the present laws were about right. "Welfare state"
is what semanticists call a slur word, and repels most
Americans. But specific programs, like old-age pensions
and medical care, which are referents for the abstract
term, are widely approved.

Bringing the matter up to date, Gallup asked in 1961,
"Do you favor or oppose additional social security taxes
to pay for old-age medical insurance?"[8] Sixty-seven percent of all adults favored additional taxes; 69 percent 50
years or older favored them. Only about a quarter of the
U.S. population was opposed. Gallup reports that those
who were against the project seldom gave "socialized
medicine"—another slur word—as a reason.

Here is a curious reaction to an economic question
asked in 1961: "Do you consider that the amount of federal income tax you pay is too high?"[9] One would expect
99 percent to vote yes. Gallup found, however, that only
46 percent of us felt our taxes were too high; 45 percent
felt the assessment was about right; while one percent
maintained the tax was too low!

HAZY DEFINITIONS

For many Americans in the upper brackets, the economy is known as "our free enterprise system." But when a nation-wide sample of adults was asked to define "free enterprise," less than a third had an adequate answer, while many told the interviewer that it meant something given away free—like premiums at a sale.

A 1960 poll showed that only one worker out of four was able to explain the meaning of "capitalism," as an economic system based on private ownership.[10] Large majorities were unable to define "socialism," "technology," "productivity," "depletion"; even "dividends" escaped them. Worse yet, the researchers found little difference between workers with a high school education and those with less. Economics apparently is not a favorite high school subject. A poll in 1961 found American youngsters very confused in trying to differentiate between "capitalism" and "Communism." They were against Communism, but 40 percent could not specify its disadvantages.[11]

Surveys by George Katona at the University of Michigan confirm the above.[12] Most Americans have little understanding of economics as a science, says Katona, but have considerable horse sense when it comes to economic behavior. Thus, in 1949, when the experts feared a severe recession, and said so loudly in the mass media, consumers refused to panic, went right on spending, and so checked the downswing. Again, in 1958, heavy spending for nondurable goods kept the recession of that year within bounds. We will return to the Katona surveys presently, as they illustrate one of the outstanding achievements of opinion measurement.

BIG BUSINESS

In late 1959, Gallup asked this question: "Which carries the greatest threat to the economy?" Respondents lined up as follows: [13]

Big Labor	41%
Big Business	15
Big Government	14
D.K.	30
	100

A strike in the steel industry at the time may have generated some bias against the unions, but it is clear that Big Business is no longer the monster it used to be. Before World War I the "trusts" were often depicted in the cartoons of the yellow press as overfed gentlemen in plug hats with dollar signs all over their vests, making off with pieces of the public domain.

The percentages also make it clear that "Big Government" is taken in stride by most Americans. We worry, however, about Big Labor, especially Mr. Hoffa of the teamsters' union. The report concludes: "Most people accept bigness as inevitable and believe abuses will be corrected."

Roper, in a 1960 television program, expanded this attitude with the following observation:

The public is not opposed to bigness. The public rather likes bigness. We've done surveys . . . on big

business, and we find that overwhelming majorities of
the public expect that large corporations, rather than
small, will make the best inventions, will give the
best merchandise for your money, will give the best
values, will pay labor the best wages, will give a man
greater job security if he works for them. The public is not opposed to bigness. The public is opposed to
the misuse of bigness.

Katona tends to confirm Gallup and Roper. The New
Deal attack on money changers and profiteers, he says, is
almost forgotten. Many respondents believe that Big
Business helps avert depressions—though more of them
credit Big Government for this. Only a minority charges
Big Business with the responsibility for inflation. Monopoly and collusion are seldom mentioned.

The public believes, says Katona, that competition exists
broadly throughout the economy, though not of the old
cutthroat variety. People think of choosing between a
Ford and a Chevrolet; they think of shopping around Supermarket A compared with Supermarket B.

There is some ideological objection by consumers to
"bigness" as such, Katona reports, but it does not influence
action. People buy willingly from Detroit car makers and
other big firms. People tend to trust well-known brands,
which are usually the product of big firms. They say that
they are pleased when their sons get jobs with Jersey
Standard, or General Electric, or other giant corporations.

A Gallup poll in 1956, however, indicates that there is
some fear that Big Business can be overdone.[14] Question:

"There has been a tendency for big companies to get bigger. How do you feel about it?" Thirty-seven percent said it was a good thing, while 46 percent felt it was a bad thing for firms to go on expanding. The rest didn't know.

In summary, the poll takers find that the majority of Americans either approve Big Business or tolerate it. But *Look* reported in 1960 that *two-thirds of all American men would rather be their own boss than work for a corporation.*[13] Respondents might be pleased to have their sons on the pay roll of the Telephone Company, but personally they preferred independence.

REGULATION OF BUSINESS

The polls to date show little public demand for more regulation of business, which seems to confirm the anti-socialist position. "Most people," says Katona, "know of no specific evils which would make the introduction of controls over business necessary."

At the end of World War II, however, as noted earlier, a large majority (77 percent) was in favor of holding price controls for a while, and only three percent felt that price ceilings were a bad thing.[15] Congress disagreed, and dismantled the Office of Price Administration on the argument that competition would hold prices in line. Prices, however, rose consistently, suggesting that the people were right in their fear of inflation after the war.

Fortune, in October, 1948, asked Americans what they thought of the regulation of business by government at that time. It is carried too far, said 37 percent; not far enough, said 21 percent; about right, said 27 per cent. In

1957 a Roper poll asked the same question and got a par-
allel result: [16]

Regulation is carried too far	34%
Not far enough	17
About right	34
D.K.	15
	100

Far from demanding more regulation of business—as,
for instance, by stiffer antitrust laws—twice as many respondents wished to reduce it.

When the country was sliding into a recession in 1958,
the public was asked: "Which one of these things do you
think is the most important step that should be taken to
combat the recession?" [17]

Unions should not ask for wage increases	32%
Government should act to check it	29
Corporations should lower prices	18
People should buy more	6
D.K.	15
	100

The accent was on government action and self-denial
by the unions. Self-denial by business ranked third. What
really checked the recession, however, as Katona pointed
out, was not that people bought *more*, but that they went
right on buying.

CONSUMER ATTITUDES

Katona and his staff at the University of Michigan have conducted more than 50,000 interviews with consumers since 1946, many at the request of the Federal Reserve Board following the war. The results comprise the largest collection in the country covering basic information about the opinion and behavior of American consumers.[12]

As a statistical group, says Katona, consumers are less inclined to economic excess than business executives. The latter tend to overexpand investment in good times, and overretrench in bad times. Consumers thus act as a kind of balance wheel for the economy, operating on the philosophy that "what goes up must come down," and help to hold inflation to the creeping, rather than the galloping, variety.

As a result of these 50,000 interviews, Katona concludes that American consumers possess a hidden wisdom which keeps the economy in balance. He does not evaluate, however, the *kind* of goods and services which comprise this balance. Other students, such as J. K. Galbraith, have raised serious questions about the benefits to the consumer of some of the goods and services consumed.

In this connection, the following question on a nationwide poll is pertinent: "Suppose you won $2,500 in a quiz show with the tax already taken out—but with the provision that you had to *spend* it—you couldn't invest or save it. What things on this list would you be most apt to use the money for?" [18]

Down payment on a house, said	42%
Vacation and travel	27
New furniture	25
A car	23
Outlay for education	20
Clothing	18
Kitchen appliances	10
Hi-fi equipment	6

(Percentages add to more than 100 because many people gave more than one answer.)

DEBT AND INSTALLMENTS

Katona reports two nation-wide polls as follows under this head:

	1954	1959
Favor installment buying	50%	60%
Oppose it	37	32
Undecided	10	7
D.K.	3	1
	100	100

A majority of American families now carry some kind of installment credit. The buying of cars, washing machines and back-yard swimming pools on credit is accepted almost as readily as buying a home with the help of an FHA mortgage. But citizens are vague about the *rate* of interest they pay; cost is not the crucial consideration.

One American in 10 believes it morally wrong to go into debt. It would be interesting to compare this result with a scientific sample taken in 1850, or in 1800. I suspect that a far higher percentage of citizens would have been morally shocked in the early years of the Republic. Installment buying is a debt, often with ferocious and hidden interest charges, but opposition is crumbling, especially since the war. Sixty percent of us approved this kind of debt in 1959 against 50 percent in 1954.

Katona reports that 12 percent of U.S. families in 1960 were "overextended" because of installments. This is a long way from the situation feared by some alarmists, in which a majority of Americans stagger under monthly payments out of all proportion to their income. During the five years to 1961, installments have stabilized at around 10 percent of the borrower's family income.[19] If income was, say, $6,000, unpaid installments averaged $600.

Installment credit is concentrated in the middle-income brackets—$5,000 to $10,000 a year. Families with less than $2,000 are mostly free of installments; families with more than $10,000 mostly pay cash. Buying goods on installment is thus primarily a phenomenon of the American middle class.

Most respondents, says Katona, believe that annual models of cars and other durables offer real improvements in function as well as in appearance. The decisions in buying durable goods, he finds, are usually made *jointly* by husband and wife. How the family income shall be spent is not a major source of matrimonial conflict, respondents say.

Meanwhile, there is little question that liberal consumer credit—that is, going into debt—has raised American living standards, so far as material things are concerned. "The American people," someone once said in a statement which has become a classic, "do not run around in 60 million motorcars because they are prosperous; they are prosperous *because* they run around in 60 million motorcars."

Opinion surveys show that the rich are no longer the pace setters for new products and luxuries in America. Families in the middle brackets are the style leaders today, according to Katona, buying, with the help of installment credit, new gadgets for the kitchen, household, and garden; buying outboard motors, fur coats, vacation package tours, and, of course, the latest in motorcars. "In the past few decades, many new and generally accepted ways of living have started outside upper-class homes." This shift, I believe, is unprecedented in economic history.

CONSUMER SAVINGS

One might hazard a guess that monthly payments on consumer credit would absorb all the family savings. On the contrary, the Katona surveys show that installment buying tends to encourage more thrift. "The $72.16 a month on the car keeps me from throwing money around." People force themselves to save, taking their personal temptations into consideration. "I'll buy a house—or a car, or a deep freeze—and then by jiminy I'll *have* to save $72.16 a month!" There is not a great deal of impulse buying, Katona finds, but plenty of "keeping up with the Joneses."

In 1940 the liquid assets of all U.S. families were estimated at $45 billion; in 1960 at $200 billion, indicating a huge increase in savings in 20 years. Despite the boom in common stocks since 1950, most people feel that stocks are "risky," and put their money into savings banks, government E bonds and insurance. A sample of 4,773 families in 1960 showed that slightly more than 14 percent owned marketable common stocks, compared to 10 percent in 1955. One third of these families, however, had invested less than $1,000 in stocks; two-thirds less than $5,000. At the other extreme, the Katona sample showed that one family in 50 owned stocks worth $25,000 or more.

Most Americans say they are not interested in saving to accumulate a fortune; only five percent mention this goal in the $10,000-a-year-and-up group. People save for:

Insurance against disaster and emergencies
Education for the children
Retirement
Buying a house some day
Starting a small business

The family car is not regarded as an asset but as current expense, like groceries, clothes, and a TV set. The family car has not been regarded as a luxury since the 1920's.

Social security, instead of weakening the willingness of Americans to save—as widely predicted—seems to have had the opposite effect. It has made people security conscious, and instead of a little of it they want a really adequate amount. Before the social security laws were passed in the 1930's, poor people had little interest in, or hope of, financial security. Now the lower income groups are keenly aware of it.

INFLATION

Polls indicate that the fear of inflation is vague; most people feel it is bad, the way "spending" is bad—and say so in a stereotyped response. A 1959 survey found less than 50 percent of us worried about continuous creeping inflation.[20] Only a minority expected higher prices five years hence—in 1964. The subject seems misty in the public mind today, contrasted with sharp anxiety during World War II. Respondents often say that American businessmen are more interested in stable prices than in continually rising prices, and people still show faith in the power of competition to restrain the cost of living. "In recent years," said Rensis Likert, "the large majority of Americans felt no doubt about the long-run stability of the value of the dollar."

In a recent Roper poll, however, about a third of respondents believed that inflation was a major economic problem.

So far as the responsibility for high prices goes, a 1961 survey is reasonably impartial: [21]

Labor is to blame	31%
Management is to blame	26
Both are to blame	29
D.K.	14
	——
	100

In this poll, respondents were most disturbed by high food prices, next by high medical costs. They seemed to have a pretty firm grip on the spiral of inflation—higher wages lead to higher prices, which lead to higher wages, ad infinitum. Twenty-nine percent of respondents blamed both labor and management.

During the steel strike in 1959 people were asked: "Do you think the steel industry could or could not afford to give the workers a raise without increasing the price of steel?" [22] Twice as many respondents thought the steel industry could afford it as thought it could not. The public, of course, had no access to the books of the steel industry, but seemed to be reflecting a rather emphatic prejudice— which may also be significant.

In summary, the polls bring out the unprecedented conclusion that the middle class is the style leader in new products in America today. The rich have lost their pre-eminence in this department. Most of us think of our-selves as members of the middle class, upholding the middle way. Broad social security programs are approved; public ownership of the means of production—except for public utilities—tends to be disapproved. Socialism, which had some appeal in the depressed 1930's, is now rarely considered. Communism is beneath contempt.*

The American folklore about the evil of going into debt is softening under the impact of installment buying. Social security has encouraged savings by making all of us secu-rity conscious. Thus, traditional economic standards are undergoing far-reaching changes. Whether the emerging system is an improvement is for the reader to decide.

* For more reactions to Communism see Chapter 10, Civil Liberties.

6
WORK

Most American men, as we noted in the last chapter, quoting a Gallup poll, would rather be their own boss than work for a corporation. At the same time, these respondents were pleased when a son secured a job with a big company. Two-thirds of all young Americans, 14 to 22, in a 1961 poll "would rather work for a large corporation than start their own small company." [1] There is obviously a conflict between motives of independence and security in the workaday world.

Work patterns, like everything else today, are under pressure from technological change. The robot on the assembly line has been with us ever since Henry Ford began mass producing automobiles. There has been a massive relative shift from agricultural work to industrial work, and lately from industrial work to the so-called tertiary or service trades. These last now account for more

than half of all the gainfully employed in the United States
—clerks, professional people, government people, sales-
men, home service men, et cetera. Now comes automation,
where a new kind of machine, equipped with a feedback
device, invades not only industrial work, like the refining
of oil, but many kinds of bookkeeping, recording and
clerical work. Some observers call automation the "second
industrial revolution."

In this chapter we will gather a variety of opinion on
conditions of work today. How do people like their jobs?
What would they rather be doing? What do they think
of unions? If they are on the assembly line, how do they
enjoy it? How do they feel about automation?

ATTITUDE TOWARD UNIONS

Of 70 million Americans gainfully employed—or seeking
to be—only about 18 million belong to a labor union of
any kind, roughly one in four. Despite this low ratio,
union members have enormous strategic power in the
national economy. A railroad strike, a steel strike, a milk
drivers' strike, can tie the community into knots. We remember the poll in *Look* which showed that citizens were
more afraid of Big Labor—and note the adjective *big*—
than of Big Business or Big Government.

Despite this fear, the majority of the public, according
to Gallup, has never been antiunion in 25 years of opinion
surveying. Here are three samplings on the subject: [2]

"In general, do you approve or disapprove of labor
unions?"

	Feb. 1957	Feb. 1959	May 1961
Approve	76%	68%	63%
Disapprove	14	19	22
D.K.	10	13	15
	100	100	100

Percentages shift with the news; a bad strike reduces the approval figure, but that figure has not dropped below 60 percent in recent years. It was relatively low in May, 1961, because of a current strike in the construction of missile bases. The all-time high, Gallup reports, was 76 percent in February, 1957. "Disapproval" of unions has seldom exceeded 20 percent. Before World War II, however, a series of strikes in defense industries raised disapproval to 30 percent.[3]

It is interesting to note how, in 1961, class and occupation influence the respondents' view of labor unions:

	Approve	Disapprove	D.K.
Unskilled workers	79%	11%	10%
Skilled workers	75	12	13
White collar	65	23	12
Business and professional	64	24	12
Farmers	56	22	22

Many unskilled workers, still presumably unorganized, hoped to join a union, which may account for the high approval. Farmers registered the lowest rate of approval, but it was still more than 50 percent, with 22 percent undecided. (Note that all figures across add to 100.)

FEATHERBEDDING

We may approve of the principle of labor unions but we strongly disapprove of featherbedding.

"In order to create work some unions require more workers than are actually needed on a job. Would you favor or oppose laws to stop this practice?" [4] Fifty-four percent of a nation-wide sample favored such laws in 1959; 26 percent, about half as many were opposed. Twenty percent didn't know.

In May, 1961, the public line was even tougher: "Would you favor jail sentences for labor leaders who require employers to hire more workers than are needed?" [2]

	In defense industry	In any industry
Favor jail sentences	53%	41%
Oppose	23	35
D.K.	24	24
	100	100

Thus, Americans are not too sure about sending union leaders to jail for featherbedding as a general proposition— 41 percent yes, 35 percent no—but a majority believes it the proper thing to do in defense industries.

In the above survey, Gallup also asked people what they thought in general about laws regulating trade unions. Forty-six percent thought the laws were not strict enough; 25 percent thought they were about right; only eight percent considered present union regulation "too strict."

"Should unemployment benefits be paid to workers who go on strike?" [5] This was asked back in 1949. Sixty-nine percent of respondents were against paying benefits to strikers; 20 percent were in favor.

In 1959 Gallup polled a nation-wide sample about compulsory arbitration for union-management disputes—a procedure where both sides must accept the ruling of a special court, and heatedly opposed by most union leaders.[6] Fifty-nine percent of the public favored compulsory arbitration; 21 percent opposed it; 20 percent didn't know. A steel strike was in progress at the time, which may have increased the vote in favor.

It is reasonably clear, from the above series of surveys, that while the public approves the principle of trade unions, it is dubious about performance, especially in respect to featherbedding.

A survey of union leaders by the National Labor Service in 1959 showed 94 percent of them believing that Negroes should be given full rights in unions and in opportunities for job promotion; 80 percent approved integrated schools, where Negro and white children sit side by side.[7]

MINIMUM WAGES

When the bill for a national minimum wage of 40 cents an hour first came up in Congress in 1938, 59 percent of the public approved.[8] Eleven years later, in 1949, 68 percent approved a higher minimum wage of 75 cents. In 1954 the one-dollar minimum was backed by 60 percent of U.S. adults. A further increase up to $1.25 an hour was proposed in 1961, with the following reaction:

	National Total	Blue collar	White collar	Professional	Farm
Favor the increase	76%	88%	83%	68%	49%
Oppose it	18	8	13	24	38
D.K.	6	4	4	8	13
	100	100	100	100	100

Here is a very interesting spectrum by occupations. As a people we are strongly for an increase in the legal minimum wage—76 percent of us. Blue collars or manual workers are 88 percent in favor; they are the class most affected. White collars, with many poorly paid clerical jobs, are 83 percent in favor. Then comes a sharp drop in approval to 68 percent by professional people, and an even sharper drop by farmers—some of whom, one suspects, are loath to increase the cost of farm labor. More farmers approved, however, than disapproved—49 percent to 38.

"Do you think a revival of the CCC camps [Civilian Conservation Corps, the most popular of all New Deal measures] a good idea?" [9] Gallup asked this in August, 1961, when Americans were concerned both with the Peace Corps proposal of President Kennedy, and the mounting problem of juvenile delinquency. The result was high approval—80 percent of us thought a revival of the CCC a good idea; 13 percent a poor idea. But when we were asked if idle young men should be *required* to go to a CCC camp, approval dropped sharply to 59 percent. Thirty-four percent disapproved the idea, seven percent didn't know.

During a business recession, which class of workers suffers most? A survey by the University of Michigan, concerned with the facts of the 1958 recession, found an answer.[10] Four in 10 of unskilled workers said they had lost their jobs, three in 10 of skilled workers, two in 10 of those furnishing services, one in 10 of clerical and sales people. Here is another interesting spectrum. It shows the vulnerability of one's job to the business cycle.

TREND TOWARD AUTOMATION

Certain observations by Professor Bernard Karsh before the annual meeting of the American Sociological Association in 1960 are significant in this connection.[11] He believes that technological changes soon will make our industrial system as different from the present, as the present is different from that of the nineteenth century. The United States, he says, has become the first industrial society in which white-collar workers outnumber blue-collar. Between 1952 and 1959, there was a 60 percent increase in professional and technical workers in manufacturing, an 11 percent increase in clerical workers in factories, while semiskilled workers declined five percent, and unskilled workers 12 percent. Computers and mathematical concepts, said Professor Karsh, are revolutionizing methods of decision-making and control. Census projections show professional and technical employees increasing their numbers by one half in the decade to 1970, while blue-collar workers will continue their relative decline.

Increased numbers of clerical workers do not necessarily

mean higher or more responsible positions. A survey by the University of Michigan of 2,300 workers affected by office automation in 1960 indicates an increase in centralized decision-making due to computers.[12] "Rules and regulations are substituted for individual decision-making. . . . Previously this function had supported the white-collar worker's claim to status. . . . Long service employees were stripped of many of their responsibilities at a time when the right to make such decisions was the principal reward of the job." Automation resulted in more decisions by top executives, fewer by the lower echelons, leading to increased resentment.

SATISFACTION ON THE JOB

This brings us to the important question of people's feelings about their work.

A Roper poll in 1957 showed a sharp contrast between what an American boy hoped to do when he grew up, and what he actually did: [13]

	Childhood ambition	Present job
Hoped to be a professional man	18%	6%
Military or railroad man	14	13
Farmer	10	13
Mechanic, not in factory	7	19
Artist of some kind	3	1
Small businessman	2	7
White-collar worker	2	15
Factory worker	1	15

The boy's ambition to be a doctor or an engineer was disappointed, three to one. So was his ambition to be an artist. The jobs he did not much care for were those he mostly landed in.

Some polls indicate that the majority of respondents like their present jobs, and if they had to choose again would follow the same occupation. A University of Michigan survey finds three out of four satisfied with their present progress on the job, and a majority satisfied with their present income.[14] But there is another way to interpret these figures. They may reflect not so much real satisfaction, as protection of the respondent's ego. He may be loath to admit that he is not doing well; thus a psychological bias may get into the percentages. This possibility is supported by the Roper poll above:

Present occupation	Would you choose it again?
Professional	Yes, 72%
White collar	51
Small business	50
Farmer	50
Blue collar—not in factory	37
Blue collar—factory	30

Professional people seem well satisfied; white collar, small businessmen and farmers are fifty-fifty. The majority of blue-collar workers, however, are not satisfied, and do not mind saying so in this survey. I would credit it ahead of other surveys which show high satisfaction on the job.

Most anthropologists agree that man, biologically, is a working organism; his opposed thumb and relatively big brain, his curiosity and energy, drive him to activity, physical or mental, or both. For normal people, just sitting around doing nothing will eventually lead to intolerable boredom if not mental breakdown. A survey I participated in, where we questioned former employees who had retired from a large company at 65, demonstrated the point.[15] Unless a retired man had a hobby, or a part-time occupation of some sort, he was likely to be in trouble. We found one chap so distraught that he would go to the shop every day and watch younger men do what he used to do. Others underwent a more or less serious mental breakdown.

There is work and work, to be sure. One man's enjoyment may be another man's misery. Work in a high-energy culture covers a vast arc, from the repetitive motions of the man attaching the rear bumper on a car to the excitement of a physicist preparing to put a man on the moon. Perhaps no more dreary labor was ever conceived than the featherbedding practice once common in the printing trades, where compositors reset, by hand, copy already printed by machine, their useless type presently to be broken up.

High-energy conditions, as Professor Karsh pointed out, call for relatively more scientists, technicians, specialists, and relatively fewer farmers, miners, factory workers, unskilled laborers—with automation speeding the process. It

would be logical to expect serious dissatisfaction among
those whose jobs are on the way out, or who are forced
to abandon responsibility and decision-making to a machine, and there is evidence to verify this expectation in
a number of research surveys. We will present two: the
job in Plant 5, and the man on the belt in a Connecticut
automobile factory.

THE JOB IN PLANT 5

Here is a large manufacturing company, with 500 employees in Plant 5.[16] They are both skilled and semiskilled
workers, producing a quality product. Wages are good,
shop conditions up to date, fringe benefits liberal; man-
agers even take courses in human relations. Although
there is no union, grievances, absenteeism, turnover, are
low. There is not much scrap and waste, little stealing,
little breaking of shop rules. In brief, Plant 5 is a long way
from the "dark satanic mills" of the nineteenth century.
It appears an industrial Utopia at first glance.

But let us glance again. When these 500 men were
carefully interviewed from the standpoint of job satisfaction, a most significant conclusion appeared. The results
of preliminary top-of-the-mind interviews were widely
at variance with the results of more intensive depth interviews. On the top, everything seemed fine, underneath the
surveyors found serious if not dangerous frustration. If the
interviewers had stopped at the top, their picture of Plant
5 would have been very wrong indeed.

In preliminary interviews, 92 percent of the men testi-

fied that Plant 5 was a good place to work, and they had
no desire to leave it. They liked the high wages and the
security. They affirmed that they were not pressured by
foremen, that management was fair, and had a right to expect plenty of hard work for a good day's pay. According
to the poll, everyone was on the team.

Now observe: when the social scientists dug deeper they
encountered a series of alarming reactions which seldom
appeared on the surface. Apathy, loneliness, even depression, were found to be wide-spread. Said one worker to
an interviewer: "There's not much to me; you might say
I'm dead." The high wages were not thought of as rewards
for production, but as the price paid for boredom and frustration. Ninety percent of the men in Plant 5 now told the
interviewers that they had no idea how management felt
about them, and they, the men, could not care less. Ninety-
six percent had no ideas for improving shop conditions or
methods; 77 percent aspired to no positions of responsibility; and 65 percent reported no personal satisfaction in
their work; "It's a job."

The workers in Plant 5 had developed a kind of creeping infantilism, for which the surveyors blamed the pyra-
mid structure of the company, with most decisions at the
top. At lower levels the mind went to sleep. "The only
satisfaction around here, Doc, is the old buck."

This important survey should be a warning not only to
employers, but to poll takers.

ON THE BELT

Charles R. Walker and Robert H. Guest, in a study of
1,800 assembly line workers in a Connecticut automobile
plant, strongly support the Plant 5 conclusions.[17] "Roughly
10 percent of our sample of workers preferred, or were
indifferent to, jobs with mass-production characteristics,
such as mechanical pacing, repetitiousness, and so forth.
The great majority expressed in varying degrees a dislike
of these features of their job situations." The belt was resented nine to one.

The investigators found that the assembly line man is
deprived of normal work satisfaction in two important
respects. First, work is all preplanned for him; he just
briskly attaches the windshield wiper as the car goes by.
He has no responsibility for the pace of his work or its
content. In the second place, he works alone with almost
no chance for teamwork with others. The others are there,
up and down the line, but he has no direct connection
with them, no group feeling. The belt weakens the individual's sense of belonging to a working community. The
mind is lulled, or harbors, in some workers, increasing
frustration. "We suggest that the sense of becoming de-
personalized . . . is for those who feel it, a psychologically
more disturbing result than either the boredom or the
tension."

"If you can daydream it isn't so bad," said one worker.
The survey showed, too, that the men hated being paced
by a machine rather than by their own working rhythm.
"The guys yell 'Hurrah!' whenever the line breaks down;

you can hear it all over the place." Many said that they were bored to the limit of endurance. "The job is so sickening, day in and day out plugging in ignition wires. I get through one motor, turn around, and there's another motor staring me in the face." A nightmare image.

The men said they had no chance to develop personal skills, and this made them feel stupid and inferior. "There is no figuring it out for yourself; no chance to use your brain." They worked in a kind of mental twilight zone. Attention must be paid, but not enough attention to interest them. A job, men said, which freed the mind completely would be better, but a job which really engaged the mind was best of all. The craftsman in them was in revolt.

The men on the belt had few grievances against their foremen, the equipment, or the plant. The washrooms were clean, the light was good. But their frustrations came out in various little things they said about "the Company," off there in Detroit. They had to blame somebody for their unhappiness.

Walker and Guest found that when assembly line workers joined a union, some sense of group participation was restored. This would seem to be an important function of the union in a world of de-personalized jobs.

ADVICE TO THE YOUNG

In March, 1949, Gallup asked this question: "Suppose a young man came to you and asked your advice about taking up a profession. Assuming he was qualified, which one of the following would you first recommend to him?" [18]

A doctor, said	27% of respondents
An engineer	17
Businessman	10
Lawyer	8
Government man	7
Professor or teacher	6
Clergyman	5
Banker	3
Dentist	3
Editor (newspaper)	2
Druggist	1
Veterinarian	1
D.K.	10
	100

Below is advice from a different angle. A 1956 Minnesota poll asked: "Suppose someone came to you for advice about which of two jobs to take, both offering the same starting salary and working conditions. One job is with the federal government, the other in a private business concern. Which job would you advise him to take?" [19]

	Men respondents	Women respondents
With the government	46%	53%
With the business firm	41	28
D.K.	13	19
	100	100

If Big Business is no longer the monster in the public mind it used to be, neither is "Bureaucracy." With men respondents, the choice between the government job and the private job was fairly close—46 percent to 41. Women respondents, however, preferred the government job by almost two to one—53 percent to 28.

Why? Probably because of the security it offered. Security is bound to be eagerly coveted in a culture where rapid technological change puts so many kinds of work in jeopardy.

7
POLITICS

Most people associate polling with elections and politics, and this, as we have seen, is only part of the story. Nevertheless, public attitudes toward politics can tell us a great deal about the processes that go on in our democracy, not only in voting but in voters' minds. We shall find in this chapter a disquieting amount of ignorance and apathy on the part of the sovereign citizen. Depressing as these facts may be, we must face them, if we hope to understand American credos. Fortunately, there are also certain offsets and compensations to be found.

THE IDEAL VOTER AND THE ACTUAL

The deep and persistent gulf between theoretical democracy and the political behavior of most Americans comes to light in many careful surveys. One memorable study concludes that it is just as well we do not live up to the elevating theories. In 1954, Berelson, Lazarsfeld and McPhee published their famous analysis of voting behavior in Elmira, New York, using the panel method of opinion research.[1] Citing Locke, Burke, Hobbes, Bentham, Mill, and other classic authors, the study lists four political duties of citizens in a theoretically perfect political democracy:

1. Their interest in politics should be strong.
2. Their knowledge of issues should be competent.
3. Their political principles should be cherished and conscientiously acted upon.
4. Their political behavior should be guided by reason and logic.

Unless a majority possesses these virtures, according to the classical school, democracy cannot function effectively.

How did the citizens of Elmira meet the test? A panel of 1,000 voters, interviewed and reinterviewed over many months, was found to lack all four virtues by substantial margins.

1. As a statistical group, they exhibited little sustained interest in politics.
2. Their knowledge of issues was rudimentary.
3. Their political principles were hard to locate—beyond voting the way their fathers did.
4. Reason and logic were far from their minds as they entered the polling booth.

There is excellent reason to suppose that this panel of voters in Elmira was a fair sample of voters the country over. Most of us fail to meet the four classical standards. American democracy, accordingly, should be dead as a dodo. Actually, it is very much alive.

Why? The authors of *Voting* advance the following arresting hypothesis. If we all followed the classical injunctions, they say, we would take our political principles very seriously, with a strong ideological bias. No loser in an election would send a telegram of congratulations to the winner. Not only slogans would be hurled at the opposition, but brickbats and even bullets, and our democracy would be in danger of dissolving in a national Donnybrook Fair. In some Latin American countries citizens *do* take their politics so seriously that fatalities often disgrace big elections and democracy is anything but stable.

The die-hard conservatives, the apathetic, and the energetic reformers provide enough consensus, these authors say, to hold the American system together, and enough cleavage to make it dynamic. Too much consensus would be deadening; too much cleavage would be destructive. "Total" politics leads to one-party government, where the opposition is banished if not shot. Total apathy could lead to a closed society, too, as a strong man takes over.

The Elmira study concludes that Americans have evolved a workable medium, a kind of political mulch, in which democracy can grow. If this judgment is sound, it is destined greatly to change our ideas about the structure of democracy, and to form one of the few substantial additions to political theory since the close of the eighteenth century. Without the young science of opinion research, this fertile new theory with its statistical backing could hardly have been developed.

A poll of 525 registered voters in 1961 in New Haven,

Connecticut, goes far to support the Elmira conclusions.[2] Participation in local political decisions was found to be apathetic by most voters, the well-to-do taking slightly more interest than the less prosperous. "The sources of the myth about the primacy of politics in the lives of the citizens of a democratic order are ancient, manifold and complex . . . deriving from the Greek city state. Whether the citizens of Athens were, in fact, more highly concerned with public affairs than the citizens of New Haven, we shall probably never know."

The study concludes that in New Haven the central fact of political life is that politics—local, state, national, and international—lies for most voters at the periphery of attention, interest, and activity. "At the focus are food, love, sex, family, work. . . ."

IGNORANT VOTERS

A good deal of evidence in other surveys bears out the Elmira and New Haven conclusions. Hyman and Sheatsley noted that during the campaign of 1948 10 percent of U.S. voters did not know who was running for President, and only half could name the vice-presidential candidate of either party.[3] About two-thirds of us had no knowledge of party platforms nor the foggiest idea where candidates Truman and Dewey stood on important issues.

A survey of the 1958 elections found that only half the voters could name at least one of the candidates for Congress they were supposed to be voting for.[4]

"One of the remarkable constants in every election campaign," observes Roper, "is that portion of the citizenry which answers a bland 'I don't know' to questions of crucial political importance." [5] As the 1960 presidential campaign began, 24 percent of respondents in a Roper poll reported they were "not much interested yet"—the same percentage as in 1956. Twenty-eight percent could not name the Democratic candidate for Vice-President (Johnson); 33 percent could not remember the name of the Republican candidate (Lodge). Six percent of our sovereign citizens could not name *any* candidate for President or Vice-President. When asked what *issues* concerned them in the 1960 election, 32 percent could think of none.

In 1948 a leading poll taker asked: "Can you tell me what the main job of the U.S. State Department is?" [6] Only a third of respondents gave the correct answer. Twelve percent gave an incorrect answer; 55 percent admitted they did not know.

Earlier, the same organization asked respondents if they had ever heard of the U.S. Foreign Service. [7] Thirty-eight percent said that they had, 53 percent had not.

The American Voter, a book published in 1960, corroborates the political apathy found in the Elmira study. [8] It was found that:

> About 25 percent of all voters discuss politics in a campaign, and try to exert a little influence among their friends.
>
> 7 percent of all attend rallies and political dinners.
>
> 4 percent give money, buy tickets.
>
> Only 3 percent of all voters ring doorbells, use the telephone, really work.

Two-thirds to three-quarters of voters make up their minds *before* the campaign begins, but about 10 percent remain undecided until the last two weeks. This helps to account for Mr. Truman's surprise victory in 1948. In that year, incidentally, 70 percent of respondents had no idea of the provisions of the Taft-Hartley Act, a major milestone in labor legislation.

In 1952—one of the late Senator Joseph McCarthy's most active years—voters greeted the charge of Communists in government with a yawn. Why? The press and the political "pros," observe the authors of *The American Voter*, habitually overstate issues; they take far more interest in political conflict than does the public. Conflict sparks a news story; apathy on the part of the voter is frustrating to both the newspaper editor and the pros in the smoke-filled room. The practical task of the American voter is not so much to decide what policies the government shall follow, as to decide which candidate shall make policy. Thus, under our system, the winning candidate has a broad popular mandate to do about what he wants to do. The American voter is more concerned with officials than with issues, but all polls confirm that his primary concern is with personal affairs.

When the country is prosperous, the voter finds little reason to connect this happy condition with the party in power. When the country goes into a business slump, the voter begins to think it time to throw the rascals out. Homo Americanus, the authors of *The American Voter* conclude, is not a political animal. His interest in an election is primarily "who's going to win," on all fours with his interest in the World Series, the Kentucky Derby, and the annual Rose Bowl football game.

Item: One pious voter was very pleased with Mr. Eisenhower "because he is the first American President to go to church." *Item:* A lady who watched the 1956 Republican Convention on TV was perplexed at Mr. Nixon's nomination for Vice-President: "He's a foreigner, isn't he?"

The American Voter documents two large recent shifts in popular opinion, confirming what we have noted in earlier chapters. First, the philosophy of self-help, unquestioned in the 1920's, has been modified by the acceptance of government intervention in matters of social security and welfare legislation. If a political campaign today in 1962 should be based on a return to the rugged individualism of the 1920's, the appeal would be dim for the majority of voters. Second, the isolationism of the years before Pearl Harbor, the authors say, is now "outside the range of controversy."

Opinion research gives us a decidedly melancholy view of the ignorance and apathy of many voters. At the same time, it could be a useful tool in reducing ignorance. Roscoe Drummond observes: "If the President is to give greater direction to public thinking, and to fill the gaps in public knowledge, he must be aware of what the gaps are. Here some use of professional polling would be useful to provide the President with this information." [9] If public ignorance were better identified, the President could focus a news conference on ways and means to let in more light.

POLITICAL PARTIES

Most voters, say the authors of *The American Voter*, are comfortable in one party or the other by the time they are 30 years old, and pull that lever for life. This is one reason why it is so difficult to develop a strong third party in America. Three voters out of four call themselves Republican or Democrat. The allegiance, however, is formal rather than emotional. While 75 percent consider themselves members of a political party, 71 percent *of the same sample*, said that it made very little difference which party was in power. Voting is largely fixed by tradition and habit, and only a small minority, as we have seen, follows campaign arguments. The chief task of party workers in an election is to provide not arguments, but transportation.

In a muzzy kind of way, voters believe that the Democratic party speaks for the poor, the Republican party for the rich.[10] This distinction held up fairly well through the administrations of Roosevelt and Truman, but became complicated with the administration of Eisenhower. As the affluent society expands, the concept, which was never strong in the South, may evaporate altogether. In foreign policy, voters have shown a slight tendency to consider the Republican party the better defender of peace. Both world wars were fought during Democratic administrations.

More Americans now register as Democrats than as Republicans by a substantial margin, but great numbers of registered Democrats voted for Eisenhower. Research indicates that 20 to 25 percent of voters call themselves "independent," splitting their tickets, and voting for the man, not the party. Eisenhower, and Roosevelt before him, received most of this maverick vote.

IMAGES

"Do you think the parties are likely to keep their platform promises or not?" Gallup asked this just before the 1960 election, with the following result: [11]

	Will the Democrats?	Will the Republicans?
Yes, they will	44%	47%
No, they won't	34	32
D.K.	22	21
	100	100

The Republicans fared a little better than the Democrats, but the promises of neither party had the confidence of a clear majority.

Professor Samuel Edersveld conducted an interesting experiment in his classes at the University of Michigan during the 1950's.[12] Some 500 registered voters who had *not* voted in local elections for several years were divided into five groups, and urged to vote by the following methods:

Group A	Personal contact by party workers	29% then voted
Group B	Personal contact by college students	25% then voted

Group C	Personal contact by telephone	24% then voted
Group D	Received three mailings with full information on candidates	8% then voted
Group E	Received three mailings with information plus a strong moral appeal to vote	12% then voted

The professor concluded: "These findings suggest you can get the apathetic out to vote, but the only effective ways to do it are in person or by the telephone." Literature, he remarked, may serve many useful purposes, but getting out the vote is not one of them.

Leaders of both parties believe firmly that voters always want their taxes reduced. Roper, in 1953, however, found a substantial majority of American adults "against cutting taxes at the expense of external or internal security." [13] The rule was also disproved by citizens during World War II.

The *Reporter* quotes a number of citizens expressing their spontaneous opinion of campaign oratory:

Said a bartender: "You can't go by what they say in the speeches. It's bull to attract the voter; then they do what they want." Said a fat man in a candy store: "They're all a bunch of crooks, makes no difference who gets in. We're still loused up." The voter speaks, without too much affection, of "they." Not *our* party, not our leaders, not our democracy, but "they," an alien out-group.

Leo C. Stine, however, a political scientist at Western Michigan University, finds some progress on the political front in recent years: [14]

Patronage is declining; Civil Service is taking its place.

Buying votes has all but disappeared.

Big bosses are losing power.

People in need of relief or other assistance no longer must promise their vote to party leaders.

IDEAL PRESIDENT

The ideal President emerges from a series of depth interviews taken by Yankelovich for *Life* in March, 1960. In such interviews, the respondent does not answer simply "Yes" or "No;" he reveals some of the underlying reasons for his answers. The ideal President was found to be a person, or the image of a person:

Who is willing to fight for his principles, but able by conciliation to avoid a fight.

Who is above party.

Who has the common touch.

Who gets things done.

Who has had experience in foreign affairs.

Who is not motivated by personal ambition.

Among those contributing to this sample was a voter who thought Mrs. Roosevelt was a strong supporter of Mr. Nixon, and another who thought Adlai Stevenson was ambassador to Russia.

This survey raises the important question of political images. We often vote for an image in our heads, with little reference to the flesh and blood person. Hyman and Sheatsley call attention to the notorious James Curley, who was elected mayor of Boston while under criminal indictment.[3] Surveys indicated that voters regarded him as a kind of Robin Hood, who robbed the rich to help the poor. They could support this image with a clear conscience. The Dwight Eisenhower image was as politically invulnerable as that of Franklin Roosevelt. An aspiring Ph.D. could develop a fascinating thesis comparing a series of political images with the human reality.

In December, 1960, Gallup asked a nation-wide sample what living man they most admired. In spite of the voters' low opinion of politics, there were seven politicians among the first 10:

1. President Eisenhower	6. Billy Graham
2. Winston Churchill	7. Adlai Stevenson
3. Albert Schweitzer	8. Harry Truman
4. John F. Kennedy	9. Henry Cabot Lodge
5. Richard Nixon	10. General MacArthur

General MacArthur, moreover, was no mean politician —while President Eisenhower was no mean general.

PARADOX

Opinion surveys disclose many political paradoxes, but none more strange than the voters' estimate of the position and status of a public career in America today. When asked: "Would you like your son to go into politics?" two-thirds answer with a resounding "No"![3] But when they are given a list of occupations and asked to rank them, a number of public offices are close to the top—such as Justice of the Supreme Court, Cabinet member, Sen-

ator. Half the respondents in one poll believe that it is
almost impossible to go into politics and remain honest;
yet in the same survey 50 percent affirm that public office
holders in their states are doing a satisfactory job.

"If you had a son, would you like to see him go into
politics as a life's work when he gets out of school?" [15]

	Male respondents	Female respondents
Yes	30%	23%
No	58	62
D.K.	12	15
	100	100

This 1955 survey seems to contradict the one shown
earlier, where more mothers preferred their sons to go
into government service than into private business. Do
we not distinguish, however, between a ward politician
running for office, and a Civil Service employee with
plenty of tenure and security? Perhaps this explains it.

"The politician" is a stereotyped abstraction in the popular mind. Aided by the cartoonist, he normally appears
as a gross figure with an even grosser cigar, abusing a
small, meek character with a toothbrush mustache, often
clothed in a barrel and labeled "the taxpayer," or "Mr.
Citizen." When, however, specific high posts in American
society are mentioned, such as the Presidency, the Supreme Court, the Governorship, respondents are quick
to acclaim dignity and status. The abstraction is a menace,
the reality a respected necessity.

BETTER GOVERNMENT

The polls indicate that the voter, while shy of "politicians," has respect for high political office, and has sensible ideas about the conduct of government in a democratic society. Here are some examples:

"Unbalanced budget" is a slur term like "spending," with which it is, of course, allied. One would expect respondents to react against the term. Often they do, but when Roper asked a nation-wide sample in 1958 whether it was a good idea for the government to spend more than it received in times of business recession, 56 percent thought the idea was good, 33 percent thought it bad, 11 percent didn't know.[16]

If the survey is broken down by educational levels a strange and regular sequence appears:

	Grade school	High school	Some college	College graduates
Unbalanced budgets can sometimes help the U.S. economy	47%	56%	61%	73%
It is always a bad idea	37	34	33	23
D.K.	16	10	6	4
	100	100	100	100

Heavy government spending in a depression helps the unemployed, as economists know. The more limited the education, the greater the chance of unemployment, as everybody knows. Yet people with the least education in the above survey were the most convinced that unbalancing the budget was a bad idea; grade schoolers were the most conservative of the four groups. The respondents with the most education (four or more years of college—the supposed bankers, big employers and solid citizens) were the most liberal of all groups. Seventy-three percent of them favored an unbalanced budget in a time of recession, 23 percent were opposed. Interesting, and logical, too, is the way the D.K.'s recede with education—from 16 percent to 10, to six, to four percent.

Let us examine another case of support for better government. Gallup asked a nation-wide sample in 1961 if it favored extending the term for members of the House of Representatives from two years to four—a reform long advocated to allow Congressmen to spend less time campaigning.[17] A majority of respondents approved, with another significant educational spectrum:

	U.S. total	Grade school	High school	College
Approve four-year term	51%	48%	51%	57%
Disapprove	34	32	36	34
D.K.	15	20	13	9
	100	100	100	100

Again approval gains with education, and again the D.K.'s march downhill as years in school march up. Notice that approximately one third of respondents in all three groups disapprove the idea.

Now we come to an interesting popular attitude toward

health services in New York City. Hospitals, it is claimed, are having a difficult time financially in recent years, as private cancer and heart drives compete with the United Hospital Fund for contributions. A Roper survey found that respondents in New York City felt strongly "it is up to government to provide the needed funds." [18] All income brackets agreed on this. Roper concludes: "The context in which hospitals are viewed by the public has shifted from institutions deserving of community loyalty, to public services whose major financing should come from taxes."

Finally, a semantic note. If a poll taker asks the public whether "government" is spending too much or too little, the replies are likely to be dubious about more "spending." [19] But if he asks: "Would you be willing to pay more taxes for schools, or for mental hospitals, or for social security benefits," the response is likely to be affirmative. This checks with results shown in Chapter 5. Again concrete objectives prevail over abstract terms.

8

EDUCATION

Polling techniques can give us measured evidence in education, as well as in politics, about what is happening in the minds of citizens. The evidence tends to confirm some pessimistic impressions, but again there are offsets. We shall see that education is highly prized among nearly all citizens, but not for its intrinsic values of knowledge and wisdom. We shall see bleak figures which tend to show how little use many citizens make of the primary skills they have learned in school. We shall see again a striking correlation between levels of education and tolerant and liberal opinion on public issues—a correlation which would seem to be characteristically American, and to compensate for other shortcomings in our educational system—except, of course, to people who prefer intolerance.

In the preceding chapter we saw this correlation at work in connection with polls on budget balancing, and on extending the term of Congressmen. Another striking

case is the attitude toward integration, as polled by
Roper: "Was the Supreme Court's decision for racial integration in public schools a mistake?" [1]

	Yes it was
Citizens with grade school education only	40%
Some high school education	24
Some college	20
College graduates	15

More than twice as many grade schoolers as college
graduates disapproved the Court's decision.

Stouffer, in his survey of attitudes toward civil liberties
—which we will examine in more detail in Chapter 10—
went so far as to work out a "scale of tolerance" based on
education.[2] He rated college graduates at 66 percent relatively; high school graduates at 42 percent; grade school
graduates or lower, at 16 percent. "People knowing little,"
concluded Stouffer, "are ill-equipped to adjust to a world
in motion."

We saw another example in Chapter 4 when analyzing
attitudes on the United Nations. The higher the respondent's education, the more likely he was to regard the U.N.
as vital to world peace, and to wish it stronger. The better
educated were also inclined to be dissatisfied with the
current performance of the United Nations.

LEVELS OF SCHOOLING

A nation-wide sample of adults were asked in 1960
about their years in school.[3] Thirty-five percent said they
had gone no further than grade school; a few of these

presumably had not been to school at all. Forty-five percent said they had attended high school, not necessarily graduating; 19 percent said they had attended college. These people were specifically asked not to include such special training as secretarial school or art courses. The percentages probably include some bias since Americans regard education as a virtue and can be expected to give themselves credit for a maximum of virtue. At face value, nearly a fifth of us have had some college experience, fewer than half of us stopped with some high school experience. About a third of us have not gone beyond grade school.

ATTITUDES TOWARD EDUCATION

That Americans favor education for their children is readily demonstrated in the architecture of many small communities. The finest building in town is the high school —whereas in Europe it is more likely to be the church.

"Which would you say is a more important person in your community?" [4] Roper asked this question in 1950, comparing the best teacher in town with the best clergyman, with the best lawyer, the leading merchant, the best public official. The best teacher won hands down: 93 percent of the votes against four percent for the best lawyer; 50 to 35 for the best clergyman; 85 to nine for the best businessman; 70 to 20 for the best public official. Negroes in this sample showed a slight preference for the best clergyman over the best teacher; among other groups the teacher reigned supreme—the most important person in town.

A nation-wide survey in 1961 found that about half of all respondents had children of precollege age.[5] Of these parents, seven out of 10 said they expected their children to go to college, and opposed any tightening of entrance requirements. Fifty-one percent said they had already put money aside for college expenses.

A survey by the University of Michigan in 1960 was in general agreement with the above.[6] Thirty-six percent of a sample of 950 Michigan parents planned to send a child to college certainly, 18 percent might do so—a total of 54 percent. Only nine percent do *not* intend to. Here are other interesting figures in this Michigan survey:

95% of respondents believe a boy who has native ability should go to college.

44% wish college education to be financed by taxes alone—the state college idea.

23% prefer financing by families and students themselves.

26% favor using both methods.

67% are for more foreign languages in college.

33% are for more athletics and physical education.

The last two figures are significant—foreign languages taking a two-to-one lead over athletics. This may, however, show cultural bias in part; the respondent enjoys football games more than French lessons, but hesitates to say so in connection with college education.

A majority of these Michigan respondents believe that the ratio of youngsters going to college would increase sharply in the years ahead; they wanted girls to go, as

well as boys; they favored a small college over a large
one; they believed that Michigan colleges had improved
greatly in the last generation—but what else could a loyal
citizen of Michigan say?

American respect for education is manifest in the public response to federal aid to schools. Roper reported in
1960 that 73 percent of U.S. adults "think some form of
federal financing is in order." [1]

A poll in 1961 provides an interesting spectrum on federal aid, based on respondents' years in school.[7] Gallup
asked: "A bill now before the country says states can use
federal money for new buildings, or for teachers' salaries.
Which is the more important?"

	College	High school	Grade school	U.S. total
Build more schoolhouses	42%	59%	68%	38%
Increase teachers' salaries	58	41	32	26
Do both				27
D.K.				9
				100

In comparing the college, high school and grade school
percentages, this report dropped out respondents who
wanted both or didn't know, so that the figures add to
100 percent, and cannot, of course, be balanced against
the U.S. total. These proportions show dramatically that
the more schooling a respondent has had, the more importance he places on teachers' salaries, and the less on
brick and mortar. Grade schoolers on the other hand reverse the emphasis; they are for brick and mortar by two

to one. Some grade schoolers revealed a personal bias by saying to interviewers: "Teachers get paid as much or more than I do."

In the same survey Gallup asked if federal aid should go to all public schools or only to schools which were not segregated. Sixty-eight percent were in favor of aid to *all* schools, whether segregated or not. Twenty-three percent would not give federal aid to school systems where the races were segregated.

Respondents were then asked if federal aid should go to public schools only, or also to Catholic and other private schools, with this result:

	Total U.S.	Vote of Protestants	Vote of Catholics
To public schools only	57%	63%	28%
To Catholic and private schools, too	36	29	66
D.K.	7	8	6
	100	100	100

The public in 1961, however, takes a not intolerant view of federal *loans* for the construction of Catholic school buildings.[8] Forty-two percent approve such loans against 46 percent who disapprove.

In 1949, when an earlier bill for federal aid was before Congress, Catholic schools were more warmly endorsed.[9] Forty-nine percent of citizens in that year wished aid for public schools only, 41 percent for public and parochial schools, 10 percent didn't know.

Roper reported in 1960 that "inadequate educational facilities came out *fourth* on a long list of domestic problems presented to respondents.[10] Specifically, 30 percent considered it a major national problem. Obviously, federal aid to schools is very much on the public mind.

GOALS OF EDUCATION

The polls clearly show the deep involvement of Americans in education at all levels. But what do we expect from it? What values do we ascribe to school and college?

The *Look* survey of 1960 found that parents wanted their children to go to college "because it will make life easier for them." [11] Going to college to enrich one's mind was a minor consideration. This survey indicated that 78 percent of us wish we had gone further in school. Why? Because more schooling is a better road to financial success (50 percent) than is hard work (25 percent). The vote suggests a certain softening in the Horatio Alger pattern—where the young hero, with little schooling but indomitable determination, fights his way up the ladder to marry the boss's daughter.

The youngsters themselves, according to polls cited by Bredemeier and Toby, know pretty well why they go to college: [12]

> To have a good time
> To play football
> To make business contacts
> To meet attractive coeds
> To learn something

Parents do not necessarily agree, except perhaps with

the business-contact goal. College boys, parents think, get better jobs. "Most people are occupationally oriented in their evaluation of education," concludes the Michigan Survey Research Center,[6] in a burst of academic prose.

A 1959 poll by the Roper office corroborates this.[13] "A college education in the United States is now more widely regarded for its economic and status values than for the intellectual training it is supposed to afford."

In the *Saturday Evening Post's* Youth Survey of December 30, 1961, the utilitarian view of higher education was common among the teen-agers interviewed. The majority were very much aware that a degree increased purchasing power, and planned to equip themselves to bargain more effectively. Said a Florida boy: "You can be the best educated person in the world, but without a college degree you can't get a garbage man's job." In this survey:

85% of high school students want to go to college.

58% plan to go, but most of them underestimate the cost.

50% plan to work their way through college—in whole or in part.

40% think that Russian education is superior to U.S.

"In effect," says the *Post*, "they are demanding tougher education." One third of high school and college respondents, combined, had not read a book in the four months preceding the survey; half of the working teen-agers had not read one.

It is interesting to compare the ambitions of American college youths with those of students from India. University students in both countries in 1958 were asked to scale their personal aspirations.[14] The Indians—160 students in six universities—selected these five goals in order:

1. A life of service to people and nation.
2. A congenial occupation.
3. Harmonious family life, love, children.
4. The contribution of some outstanding work in the student's special field.
5. Economic security.

At the same time, more than 1,000 students in 14 American universities selected the following five goals in order:

1. Harmonious family life.
2. A congenial occupation.
3. Economic security.
4. To be liked and respected in the community.
5. Ample vacations and leisure.

Note how the goals of the American youngsters clustered around their *personal* life—family, job, security, vacations, status—while many Indian students had goals beyond their personal life: service to others, "contribution of some outstanding work to my field." More than half the Indians mentioned the desire to lead a life of service to the community, whereas fewer than 20 percent of the Americans mentioned any such idea.

George Gerbner makes the same point about American youth: [15]

Careful studies of students' attitudes show their goals in life are couched almost entirely in terms of self-reference such as personal amusement, consumption and diversion. Even among college freshmen only three percent chose usefulness to others or to one's community as an achievement to be "most proud of."

Gordon W. Allport, Harvard psychologist, writes: "The American student, by and large, manages to separate himself from the political and social context of his existence. The term *privatism* has been used to label this particular state of mind."

It is not without significance that political demonstrations abroad are often led by university students—a phenomenon rarely seen in the United States. Though these often turn into irresponsible uprisings, at least they show that the students are politically conscious. Here and there in this country, in the debate about racial integration and in some antiwar demonstrations, American college students are beginning to take a more active part in public affairs. Meanwhile, there is little to be gained by blaming our youngsters for their relative indifference. The college student in America, observe Bredemeir and Toby, learns his role from fraternity brothers, roommate, girl friend, big wheels on campus, basketball coach, parents, as well as from the learned faculty.[12] "He is not necessarily a dolt because he responds more readily to their conceptions than to ours."

When students were asked to rate their problems in a

Michigan survey in 1960, they gave top priority to choosing a good job; then preparation for marriage; then relations with their peers; then relations with parents.[16] Learning more about one's responsibilities as a citizen came far down the list.

It is interesting to extrapolate the future college population if parents' hopes are fulfilled. A Roper survey in 1959 showed that 69 percent of children now below 18 would be sent to college if parents had their way.[13] This works out to an enrollment of 11 million college students in 1970! At a modest estimate of $2,500 a year per student, the total college bill would be $27.5 billion a year, or more than $100 billion to see the youngsters through to graduation. "The public's eyes," observes Roper, "are still very much closed." The U.S. Office of Education is probably nearer the mark when it estimates 6.4 million college students by 1970.[13] But even this, at $2,500 per student, means $16 billion a year, and $64 billion for the four years.

CHOOSING A CAREER

Despite the hopes of parents and the nation-wide interest in bigger and better schools and colleges, American youngsters receive surprisingly little help from older people in choosing a career. It is up to the youngster to do his own planning—part of our cultural inheritance of self-help. One survey showed: [12]

78 percent of children in grade school had no plans for a career.

47 percent of high school students had no plans.

13 percent of college students had none.

The young people in this survey reported that they had received little advice from parents, teachers, or anyone else about future occupations. The unfortunate result, of course, is that the youngster is likely to take the first job which comes along when he leaves school.

When the impact of Sputnik I in orbit struck the United States, it started widespread concern about the state of American education. How had the Russians got so far ahead of us in space technology? Proposals were hastily advanced for better examination procedures, fewer overlapping courses, reduced teacher load, more instruction by TV, and so on.[12]

Sputnik I awakened an interest in the teaching of science and mathematics, but, as Robert M. Hutchins ironically observed, only to keep pace with Russia. "The stresses and strains in our society," he said, "are obscured for us partly by our preoccupation with Russia, which plays a curious double role of devil in our world, and as the standard by which we measure our progress. If we weren't getting ahead of Russia, or falling behind her, how could we tell where we were?"

Whatever their motives or ambitions, our young people spend many years of their lives in school and college. What do they take away? Here the polls can help us only indirectly. Graduates come out, take jobs, and presumably their schooling helps their take-home pay. The figures cited above are quantitatively discouraging, but they neglect qualitative differences. The minority who take an interest in genuine learning must include the growing body of highly educated and cultured citizens, especially in the professions. Do these people contrast so sharply with the majority as to form the beginning of an elite class? The polls I have seen throw no light on this question.

READING BOOKS

An important indirect indication of the results of education appears in many recent polls about the reading of books. As reading is the primary skill which students learn and practice throughout their school and college years, the graduates might be expected to make use of it, for business or pleasure or both, when their education is formally completed. Well, what do the polls show?

We noted earlier how American teen-agers were not precisely bookworms. In 1955, Gallup found that 61 percent of U.S. adults had not read any book, at least except the Bible, during the previous year.[17] Eighty-two percent of those who had been only to grade school could not remember reading a book on any subject during the previous 12 months; 57 percent of those who had been to high school had not read a book. Respondents who had attended college did better; only 26 percent remembered not cracking a book in the past year. Another study found that more than half U.S. citizens lived within a mile of a public library, but only 20 percent of these had entered its door during the previous year.[18]

Roper, in 1950, found 18 percent of adults who claimed

to be currently reading a book of any kind, even a cook-book.[19] The figure is probably too high, since many Americans call a magazine a "book." Another 18 percent said that they had *never* read a book that was not required for school or business. "Book reading has little status in the U.S. unless it is job-connected."

Gallup, in the same year, 1950, found 21 percent of respondents currently reading a book—a fairly good correlation with Roper.[20] By 1957, however, the Gallup percentage had dropped to 17. Could this be accounted for by the rise of television? Meanwhile, people in other countries read books by much larger percentages, according to local polls in 1957. Current readers compare as follows:

In England	55%
West Germany	34
Australia	33
Canada	31
and in the U.S.	17

It is probable that the tidal wave of paperbacks in recent years is improving the U.S. percentage. There is nothing, of course, in the inherited mentality of American children which blocks the reading of books. The attitude —like the books themselves—is all in the culture.

When mothers of preschool children were asked in what activity their children showed most interest, they reported books (presumably picture books) in second place, following the age-old pastime of playing with toys.[21] Television came third, drawing pictures fourth. Three out of four of these mothers wanted a college education for their children—the usual high percentage.

A final thought: All the surveys for the last 30 years showed roughly only one American adult out of five currently reading a book. Yet how much reading of books a citizen should do nobody knows. We assume that reading is good, and that more reading is better. So intellectuals are shocked, and then reshocked, to hear that 15 percent of college students draw no books at all from the library in a given academic year. The poll takers I think might well do two things: first, gauge the recent effect of paperbacks on these dismal figures; and second, conduct some depth interviews to correlate reading with intelligence, especially *kinds* of reading. An exclusive and voluminous diet of whodunits might boost the percentages, but would that be a real gain?

SUMMARY

"If you had your life to live over again what would you do differently?" Gallup asked this in 1953 of a nationwide sample: [22]

Get more education	33%
A different job	15
Be more tolerant	11
A different marriage situation	10
Save more money	7
Work harder	2
Travel more	2
Other goals	17
D.K.	3
	100

Education is far out in front; hard work far down the line, on a par with more travel. Horatio Alger suffers another setback.

Two conclusions stand out strongly in this record. While Americans universally favor education, wish they had had more of it, and want more for their children, the goal is primarily to improve earning power. Education for a better understanding of the world and of themselves is not often mentioned in the surveys.

In the second place, as noted earlier, despite these materialistic aspirations, the more years a citizen spends in school, the greater his tolerance tends to be, and the better his judgment.

9
SCIENCE

As science and its offspring technology continue to expand at an exponential rate, they are drastically changing our lives and calling for constant readjustment. Already civilization stands close to extinction because of the formula, $E = MC^2$, which opened the way to the nuclear bomb. The equation was in the realm of pure science, the bomb an application of it to transform matter into energy. Meanwhile, new medical discoveries, new forms of energy and materials, the distillation of fresh water from salt, offer a comparative Utopia—if the dangers of technology can be controlled. New developments in the social sciences could help us achieve this Utopia.

Science, for good or ill, is the dominating force in the world today. What does the citizen know about it? What does he think of it? What have his teachers and the mass media told him about it? How far does he realize its terrific impact on almost every phase of his personal life? In this chapter we will look for some answers to these questions, though we shall not find as many as one could wish. Opinion research has not sufficiently concentrated on this fundamental issue.

IMAGE OF "THE SCIENTIST"

For the average citizen, science is something like the air he breathes. Although the atmosphere presses down upon him with a force of many pounds per square inch, he is not aware of it. Although his life in America today would be hardly conceivable without motorcars, telephones, power lines, oil burners, elevators, subways, railroads, printing presses, television sets and electric refrigerators, he is largely unaware of the process which created the environment in which he moves and has his being.

This unawareness, I believe, is beginning to dissolve, largely as a result of the publicity given to Russian scientific advances, and the consequent shock to our national complacency. Three polls, released in 1956, 1957, and 1959, give an indication of the change. These polls unfortunately are not truly comparable, as they were taken under quite different circumstances, and we can therefore cite them only as indication, not as solid evidence.

The first, measuring the attitudes of high school students, was followed within a year by one querying their elders. Though less comprehensive than the students' poll, its conclusions were similar. The third poll, taken two years later, showed results so different as to suggest a definite shift in public attitudes.

In 1956, before Sputnik I, Purdue University released the results of a massive poll on the image of a "scientist." [1] The sample was 15,000 high school students, representing a universe of eight million youngsters all over the United States. Most of them said they would shun a career in pure science. Of 10 occupations listed, they rated atomic scientist as least desirable. A third of the students believed a person had to be a genius to be a good scientist; 30 percent thought that a scientist could not rear a normal family; 28 percent that he does not have time to enjoy life; 25 percent that scientists are typically odd-balls; 14 percent that there is "something evil" about a scientist. Nine percent believed it impossible to be both honest and a scientist. "Something seems to have gone wrong," said Purdue of this study, in perhaps the understatement of the year.

A survey made by the National Opinion Research Corporation for *Life,* in 1957, found a minority of U.S. adults sunk in ignorance of science and scientists as dark as the high school students.[2] Only 10 percent of respondents could name two living scientists. A third doubted if "scientists can be trusted with the secrets of important new discoveries"—even though it is manifest that only scientists make the discoveries. Ten percent thought American scientists are linked to Moscow, and a minority of respondents envisaged "old men with long hair and whiskers, who may be geniuses but are half-insane, keeping their heads in books all their life. . . ." This description suggests a curious throwback to the alchemists and sorcerers of the Middle Ages.

Returning to the Purdue Survey, it did contain one real-istic note. Forty-five percent of students believed that their high school background was too poor to permit them to choose science as a career.

Here are other student responses: A science teacher at Oak Ridge High School in Tennessee, the town where atomic energy was harnessed, asked his pupils, in 1958, to write down their idea of a scientist.[3] The answers were disconcerting. Scientists were people who "work with science and drink coffee." . . . They invent new "thoiries," and work on "salt vacine." . . . They are "shabby dressed," and often talk nonsense. . . . "I don't see any reason for putting a satilight up." . . . "Albert Einstein had a very low I.Q." . . . "I don't think a scientist has to be so brilliant he doesn't have any common sense." These philosophers were 14 to 16 years old.

One youngster, however, saved the day for Oak Ridge. "Without scientists," he said, "we would not have any of the modern conveniences that we have today."

A boy in Niles Township High School near Chicago took a series of intelligence tests and came out at the top of his class.[4] His father was surprised, as the boy had never reported his high rating at home. When asked about this reticence the boy replied: "I didn't want to be known as a *brain*."

We do not need polls to prove that a "brain," an "egg-head" and a "longhair" have been widely disparaged in American culture, by adults as well as high school boys.

CHANGING ATTITUDES TOWARD SCIENCE

Thanks to the Russians, the image of a scientist has shifted perceptibly. Sputnik I, launched in October, 1957, is generally credited with awakening many of us to the necessity of better education in the sciences, as noted in the last chapter. The New York State Commissioner of Education reported that thereafter the rate of program changes in New York public schools more than doubled.[5] "The schools," he said, "responded to a national need and shifted abruptly into an entirely new rate of change, and are now sustaining that rate." This conclusion is based on a questionnaire survey of 886 public school systems and 348 private school systems in the state, not including New York City. Among innovations cited by the commissioner were a new method for teaching mathematics, and improved instruction in chemistry and biology. The whole curriculum has been galvanized, he said, along with science and the social studies.

Dr. Stephen B. Withey, of the University of Michigan Research Center, published in 1959 the results of an intensive and comprehensive survey showing public attitudes toward science.[6] This came three years after the first Purdue studies, and two years after Sputnik I. It included both nation-wide and local samples of American adults. Eighty-three percent of respondents believed that the world was better off because of science; 10 percent were dubious. The beneficent effects were rated, in order: medical advances by 53 percent; higher living standards by 30 percent; increase in knowledge by only six percent.

Nuclear war was voted the number one evil effect of science. "Science destroys religion" rated far down by comparison. When asked who was responsible for the evil effects, respondents were mostly silent. Scientists were blamed by 14 percent, politicians by 12 percent, "foreigners" by six percent, the Pentagon three percent, Big Business two percent. Thus only about a third of the sample made any reply; the rest didn't know whom to blame, or considered the point irrelevant.

Advances in exploring outer space were seen more as a race with Russia than as advances in scientific knowledge—thus supporting the observation of Robert Hutchins in the last chapter. He said, you remember, that unless we were ahead of the Russians, or behind them, we wouldn't know where we were.

Now we come to a very significant series of popular reactions to science and scientists, worked out by Dr. Withey: [7]

Majorities agree that	Agree	Disagree
Science is making us more comfortable	92%	4%
Most scientists work for the common good	88	7
Scientists work harder than the average	68	25
Science promotes too rapid change	47	46 (very close)

Majorities disagree that

Scientists pry into things they should not	25	66
Most scientists are impractical	26	65
Science shatters standards of right and wrong	25	64
Scientists are likely to be religious	32	53
Most scientists are odd-balls	40	52
Growth of science means a few will control the rest of us	40	52
Science can solve our social problems	44	49 (close)

These results are a long way from the high school students polled by Purdue, and the adults queried in 1957. True, a minority of 40 percent believed that most scientists are queer fish—offset perhaps by 32 percent of respondents who believed that most scientists are religious. The vote on social science was close; 44 percent agreed that it can solve our social problems, 49 percent disagreed. The 40 percent who feared that a technocracy of scientists may some day control the rest of us could have cited an historical case. The Mayan priesthood of Mexico alone possessed the astonishing mathematics, astronomy and engineering of that society, and were the exclusive ruling class. When the Spanish conquerors eliminated the priesthood, the Maya culture lost its directing brain.

In brief, in the words of Dr. Withey: "The survey shows

there is no major emphasis on the 'mad scientist' of fiction, nor any public image of the scientist as dangerous"—except, I might add, for that fear of a dangerous technocracy. (A benevolent technocracy was once imagined by H. G. Wells. It was led by idealistic airmen, who engineered *The World Set Free*—the title of his book.)

The Michigan Center surveys show that respondents characterized scientists as intelligent, highly educated, hard working, dedicated to humanity, curious about the unknown, in that order. They downgraded a desire for money or prestige. The motivation of scientists, respondents said, was primarily the challenge of the unknown.

When asked in which of four fields scientific research should be concentrated in the years ahead, respondents answered: [7]

Medical research	54%
Research in juvenile delinquency	32
Basic work in physics and chemistry	7
Putting a man on the moon	3
D.K.	4
	100

Observe that research in juvenile delinquency lies chiefly in the field of the social, not the natural sciences. Observe, too, the relative importance attached to medical research against hoisting a man to the moon.

When respondents were asked "Who's ahead?" in 1958, they produced this significant reaction: [8]

Russian science is "greatly superior"	8%
"About the same"	26
American science is "greatly superior"	21
Russian science is better in some areas, not in others	33
D.K.	12
	100

These figures reveal both common sense and a patriotic bias. The directors of the survey observe: "It is striking that the most discriminating response was the most frequent: one person in three felt that Russian science was better in some areas, but not in others. This indicates an awareness that 'science' comprises a variety of fields. . . ." Science $_1$ is not science $_2$, as a semanticist would phrase it.

POPULAR DEFINITION OF SCIENCE

Asked to choose a definition of science, 67 percent of respondents in the Michigan survey said that it meant "thorough and intensive study" of a subject.[6] Only 10 percent chose measurement, controlled experiment, systematic variation, prediction, or other standard components of the scientific method. The popular definition thus falls far short of the true nature of science, where the findings of one competent observer can be repeated and verified by other competent observers. There can be no magic, no secret formula in true science. From Babylon to the present day, the world has produced thousands of devoted scholars who have evolved stupendous theories, but as nobody else could repeat experiments and verify results, their "thorough and intensive study" cannot be called scientific.

Respondents also lacked a clear idea of the distinction between pure science—where new laws are formulated and verified—and applied science, or technology, where a neutron bomb is manufactured or a new plastic swimming pool designed for the market. Science in the minds of most people seems to mean an artifact rather than an equation.

Fifty percent of respondents in this Michigan poll believed that scientists may study anything; 25 percent thought they should stop short of studying human behavior.[6] This is not consistent with some earlier results, and obviously the public is confused about the limitations of the scientific method in problems of human relations and behavior.

Withey found, in 1959, that 47 percent of adult Americans had had at least one course in science at high school or college, but only 11 percent had studied any science at the college level.[6] This latter proportion, though small, was increasing.

Gallup, in 1957, asked: "Would you approve or disapprove of making mathematics a *required* subject in high school?"[9] Eighty-nine percent approved, five percent disapproved. In the same survey, 66 percent approved physics as a required course in high school, 68 percent approved chemistry.

A Minnesota poll, taken in 1957, suggests why a little more instruction in science might not be a bad idea.[10] The question was asked: "Compared with the earth, about how big would you say the moon is—much larger, about the same size, or much smaller?" The sample of 600 adults replied:

Much larger	36%
About the same size	16
Total wrong	52
Much smaller	38
D.K.	10
	100

A little over one third of Minnesota respondents could size up the moon correctly—a ratio which probably applied to Americans the country over.

NEWS VALUE OF SCIENCE

Let us return to the Michigan surveys of Dr. Withey. Respondents were asked about their reactions to science news in newspapers and magazines.[11] Most readers said that they became interested in a news story when a scientist had some definite accomplishment to report—say finding a dawn man in South Africa. Stories about new laws and principles left them cold, but a claim that dolphins could talk excited immediate attention. This may help to explain why the copy desk permits so many half-baked stories to clutter news columns as "science says." Most of us like to read these fancies, but it takes more scientific background than most of us possess to recognize them as fancies. No one with knowledge of linguistics, for instance, would credit a story that dolphins could learn to talk as human beings talk. Some of the stories gave that impression.

Asked if they could recall a recent item of science news, two-thirds of respondents did so—mostly in the field of medicine, especially stories about heart disease and cancer research.[11] Nine percent had no knowledge of radioactivity, of satellites, polio or fluoridation. Only one person in six knew what all these terms meant. Popular knowledge about science, Dr. Withey concludes, runs mainly to medicine and its effect on health; indifferently to findings in the fields of physics and chemistry.

In the matter of health, Gallup has shown one way in which the polls can be of outstanding public service. In 1961 he reported the results of a survey undertaken for the American Cancer Society.[12] He was asked to find out how many women in America knew about the "Pap smear" test for uterine cancer. Uterine cancer is 100 percent curable if caught in time. Of 56 million adult females in the United States in 1961, a sample showed that 33 million had heard about Dr. Papanicolou's test. Only half that number had taken the test, which requires a simple five-minute examination. Twenty-three million women had not even heard of it. These figures gave the Cancer Society valuable information for an educational campaign.

When Dr. Withey asked respondents why they read science news in the papers, half of them replied that they wanted to keep up with what was going on in the world, while a quarter said they read because of the impact of science on their personal survival.[7]

THE GAP

C. P. Snow, who is both a distinguished British novelist and a nuclear physicist, has called the world's attention to a serious gap between persons of high intelligence trained in the humanities, and those trained in the sciences.[13] One group views the world in a way which differs alarmingly from the view of the other group. This difference is growing. "Closing the gap between our cultures," says Sir Charles, "is a necessity in the most abstract intellectual sense, as well as in the most practical. When these two cultures have grown apart, then no society is going to be able to think with wisdom."

Evidence of the gap is found in the results of a questionnaire survey conducted by Glasgow University in 1961.[14] Some 3,000 professors and students all over Britain were asked 20 questions in the arts and humanities, and 20 questions in the sciences. What famous painter had a "blue period"? . . . What scientist developed the "principle of uncertainty"? and so on.

The average performance was found to be surprisingly low. Few did well in both fields. A teachers' college, for instance, averaged 3.2 questions correct out of 20 in the humanities, and 3.7 questions correct out of 20 in the sciences. A similar study in the United States would be useful and revealing.

The image of science and scientists is changing in

America, though not so rapidly as the exponential curve of technology is changing our behavior. Nevertheless, the polls show a perceptible shift since the flight of Sputnik I. More polls are needed in this most important field.

10
CIVIL LIBERTIES

We come now to the great American heritage of civil liberties and freedoms under the Constitution. How far is the average citizen aware of them, and how does he respond to them? If we can measure this knowledge and these attitudes, we shall come as close to assessing the true "Americanism" of our people as communication and social science in their present state permit.

The heritage of civil liberty, fortunately for the opinion researcher, is expressed very concretely in a dozen amendments to the American Constitution. The first 10, adopted soon after the Constitution itself, and known as the Bill of Rights, guarantee to citizens freedom of religion, free speech, free press, freedom of assembly, and the right to petition the government for redress of grievances. The Bill of Rights protects us against unwarranted search and seizure, against having our property taken without due process of law, against double jeopardy, against being

152

forced to testify against oneself in court—the famous Fifth Amendment. It prescribes a speedy trial and the right of trial by jury; forbids excessive bail and "cruel and unusual punishment."

The Fourteenth and Fifteenth Amendments, added after the Civil War, define who is a citizen—namely, everybody born in the United States or naturalized here—and guarantee that the rights of a citizen shall not be denied because of "race, color, or previous condition of servitude." The decision of the Supreme Court ordering desegregation in the public schools was based on these constitutional provisions. We shall presently note what poll takers have found about citizens' attitudes to the desegregation decision—a measurement primarily of public prejudice. First, however, let us inspect some studies of general knowledge about Constitutional rights.

ATTITUDES TOWARD THE BILL OF RIGHTS

A summary of polls up to 1950 by Hyman and Sheatsley showed that the overwhelming majority of Americans are proud of their democracy and familiar with its idiom.[1] Majorities were strongly opposed to such terms as "Fascism," "Communism," "Socialism," "dictatorship." Our democracy is, of course, held superior to that of Britain or France. Eighty percent of us can produce a fairly good definition of "democracy," as universal suffrage, free elections, religious freedom, and so on. Only one percent of us are against "free speech" as such.

On a more specific level, however, the majorities begin to melt. In one survey reported by Hyman and Sheatsley,

31 percent of respondents said they had never heard of the Bill of Rights, while another 36 percent said they had heard the name but could not define it, and another 12 percent described it inaccurately—a total of 79 percent ignorant of this cardinal American document. Even the 21 percent who could correctly identify the Bill of Rights were not unanimously in favor of all its provisions.

Large majorities favored "free press" in the abstract, but 33 percent said they would not permit any newspaper to criticize the American form of government, and 25 percent would not let the Socialist party publish a newspaper. Seventy-five percent of us were against admitting "displaced persons" from abroad—a result probably influenced by fear of unemployment. In a list of 17 nationalities presented to respondents, only five were classed "as good as Americans," namely, the English, Canadians, Dutch, Irish, and Scandinavians. Substantial majorities, however, would give all 17 nationalities equal rights if they were here. Three quarters of respondents said that speakers on public platforms in America should not be allowed to attack other races.

Hyman and Sheatsley conclude that most of us are in favor of "freedom" as a principle, but often dubious about it in specific situations. Many respondents "tend to vote against an application of the general principle unless a reciprocal feature is dramatically brought to their attention." Thus the question: "Should Russian newsmen have freedom to report what they see in the United States?" brought out only a 35 percent "Yes." But when the interviewer explained the importance to both nations of granting freedom to the other's reporters, the "Yes" vote doubled to 70 percent.

The Purdue University survey mentioned earlier, covering high school students during the middle 1950's, found 43 percent of youngsters favoring curbs on free speech under various circumstances, and 37 percent favoring third-degree methods by the police—a practice which most jurists consider "cruel and unusual punishment." [2] Could television crime stories have biased the children's vote? A majority believed that the police should censor books, movies, radio and TV "to shield us from improper thinking." Dr. Martin Hamburger of New York University, in summarizing the Purdue findings, said: "Equality and civil liberties were not cherished by American youths to anywhere near the degree many parents and educators had assumed."

Gallup collected some interesting reactions to censorship in 1961.[3] He asked respondents what subject matter is undesirable on TV and radio, and received these complaints, in order: "excessive violence, matters not appropriate for children, too much sex, too many commercials." He then asked: "Would you approve or disapprove of more curbs on TV and radio? On newspapers?"

	TV and radio	Newspapers
Approve more curbs	49%	31%
Disapprove	39	55
D.K.	12	14
	100	100

Printed matter fares better than pictorial and spoken matter in this poll. Does it mean that the public is against "free speech" on the air? It is not so simple. There has never been absolute freedom of speech in any human community. Some utterances are almost universally taboo —for instance, "blasphemy" against the prevailing religion, pornography, incitement to violence or panic. In our culture a familiar illustration of the last is crying "fire" in a theater. The sanctions and restraints of a given culture must always be allowed for when analyzing "free speech."

A study conducted by the University of Michigan asked, in reference to presidential elections, "Where do you get most of your information?" [4]

	1952	1956	1960
From TV	31%	49%	60%
Radio	27	11	5
Newspapers	22	24	23
Magazines	5	5	4
Combination of media	9	3	3
D.K.	6	8	5
	100	100	100

TV as a source of information rises sharply while radio falls. Newspapers and magazines more or less hold their own.

A study made in 1958, by the National Labor Service at a Labor summer school, found 60 percent of union leaders ready to deny an atheist the right to teach in college; half of them would deny the right to a Socialist.[5]

Observe the heavy prejudice of labor leaders against Socialism.

MC CARTHYISM AND COMMUNISM

In 1955 the Fund for the Republic sponsored the publication of a genuine classic of public opinion research, by Dr. Samuel A. Stouffer, sometime professor of sociology at Harvard's Department of Social Relations.[6] It dealt with the activities of the late Senator McCarthy, and in general with the subject of "internal security"—namely, the danger from Communist party members and Communist sympathizers within the United States. The study was a classic not only because of the importance of its subject matter, but because of the polling techniques employed. Two major research organizations were retained to ask identical questions of different nation-wide samples, by different battalions of interviewers. Again and again the results agreed within a few percentage points. Stouffer himself was an outstanding technician in scientific polling. We have earlier referred to his study, *The American Soldier,* where careful samples told the high brass in World War II how 10 million soldiers felt about all manner of problems.[7]

"The number of people," reports Stouffer in his summary of the work on civil liberties, "who said that they were worried either about the threat of Communism in the United States, or about civil liberties, was, even by the most generous interpretation of occasionally ambiguous responses, *less than one percent.*" This came at a time when McCarthyism was at its peak in the press and on the air. Two first-class polling organizations—the American Institute of Public Opinion (Gallup) and the National Opinion Research Center (University of Chicago)—failed to discover much uneasiness in the public mind because of the charges of Senator McCarthy, or because of the fact of the Cold War with Russia.

People reported that they were interested in the *news* about these matters, but did not seem to be personally involved. Thirty percent in one poll could not identify McCarthy, or any other investigator of red activities. Only nine percent knew how Alger Hiss incriminated himself.

Stouffer noted that a "Communist" was popularly defined as:

> A person against religion.
> Who believes in government ownership.
> Is a manual worker mostly, but sometimes a bureaucrat or a professor.

Only three percent of respondents claimed ever to have known an admitted Communist, but 10 percent knew somebody they suspected might be one.

This haziness reminds me of a sidewalk poll taken by the Madison, Wisconsin, *Capital Times* in 1953, at about the same time as Stouffer's more scientific surveys. People on the street were asked, "What is a Communist?" Here are some of the replies:

> *Farmer:* "They are no good to my notion. I can't figure out what they are."
> *Housewife:* "I really don't know what a Communist

is. I think they should throw them out of the White House."

High school student: "A Communist is a person who wants war."

Office worker: "Anyone that stands for things that democracy does not."

Stenographer: "If a person didn't have a religion I would be tempted to believe he was a Communist."

Not only was there very little agreement by the people on the sidewalk, but 123 persons out of 197 interviewed frankly admitted they did not know what a Communist is. This admission came at a time when investigators in Congress were flooding the country with stories and headlines about the "Communist Menace." The Berlin crisis of 1961 again accentuated alarm in some circles about internal security and the menace of Communism. Has the average citizen today any clearer idea of "Communism" than he had in 1953? This point should be scientifically polled.

Stouffer found that community leaders tended to respect civil rights considerably more than the rank and file. He asked the question: "Should a Socialist be allowed to speak in your town?" Both polling agencies reported results as follows: [6]

	Gallup	University of Chicago
Yes, he should be allowed to speak:		
Community leaders	84%	84%
Rank-and-file in same town	60	61
Rank-and-file, nation-wide	57	60

Community leaders were thus substantially more observant of the Bill of Rights than the average citizen, but the "Yes" vote had a clear majority in all cases. Observe how close were the results of the two polling organizations, with their different corps of interviewers eliciting answers from entirely different samples. The developing science of opinion research, and the precision of its method, could hardly be better illustrated.

Earlier, we mentioned Stouffer's "tolerance index," where people with high school education were found more tolerant than those who had not been beyond grade school, and those who had been to college more tolerant than high schoolers. Community leaders, we note from the above, are more tolerant than the rank-and-file. Young people, Stouffer reported, are more tolerant than their elders. This conclusion seems inconsistent with the Purdue study, and we shall look at it more closely in a moment. The far West was the most tolerant region in respect to civil liberties, the South the least tolerant. Rural people were universally less tolerant than city people. "In the anonymity of city life, it is much easier for deviant behavior to flourish than in the goldfish bowl of a small community."

This raises a significant question. Americans today are being charged on all sides with conformity; they are called "organization men," blind followers of convention. Yet, at the same time, urban and suburban populations are growing while rural areas are shrinking. If Stouffer is right, the country should be moving toward *less* conformity, as "the anonymity of city life" makes deviant behavior easier. Not only is urban population increasing, Stouffer observes, but people are increasingly on the move from city to city in search of new jobs. This large geographical movement, along with the prevalence of motor travel, increases tolerance, he says, and encourages nonconformity, in the sense of making people less resistant to change.

RACE

How do Americans feel about integration in the schools, as ordered by the Supreme Court? We have already briefly noted, in Stouffer's educational spectrum, that college graduates are the most ready to accept integration. Now let us go into the question in more detail.

A Gallup poll in 1957, some three years after the Supreme Court order, asked respondents from the South and from the rest of the country if they approved or disapproved: [8]

	South	Southern white	Southern Negro	Rest of U.S.
Approve Supreme Court order	19%	12%	49%	69%
Disapprove	72	83	32	25
D.K.	9	5	19	6
	100	100	100	100

Negroes in the South approved the decision by a ratio of four to one over whites in the South, but their approval, at 49 percent, was not so great as that of U.S. adults outside the South, at 69 percent. Note, however, the large

D.K vote by Southern Negroes. Were many of them reluctant to answer because they feared that the interviewer at the door might pass the information on despite a pledge of secrecy? The "disapproval" of the whole South, Negroes included, was slightly more than the "approval" of the rest of the country—72 percent to 69.

Roper, in 1958, released the following figures on school integration. He compared the nation-wide vote with that of the South: [9]

	All U.S.	South only *
Schools should be integrated immediately	27%	9%
Time given to work out problem	27	15
Some day, perhaps	26	21
Never; the Supreme Court was wrong	17	52
D.K.	3	3
	100	100

In this survey, one third of all U.S. adults over 50 years of age were *against* integration, but only a quarter of respondents under 25 were opposed.

In 1961, Gallup reported that despite large unfavorable majorities, 76 percent of Southern adults now reluctantly concede that desegregation is inevitable.[10]

After the Supreme Court had ruled that segregation of races in trains, buses and waiting rooms was unconstitutional, Gallup tabulated this reaction: [11]

* Including Negroes, of course.

	All U.S.	South only
Approve	66%	26%
Disapprove	28	66
D.K.	6	8
	100	100

The "disapproval" of the South equaled the "approval" of the whole country including the South.

"Did President Kennedy do the right thing in sending U.S. marshals to Alabama to protect Freedom Riders?" (The Riders of both races rode Southern buses in 1960 and 1961.) [11]

	All U.S.	South only
He did the right thing	70%	50%
Wrong thing	13	29
D.K.	17	21
	100	100

Note the surprising 50 percent approval from respondents in the South.

When President Eisenhower sent troops to Little Rock in 1957 to prevent violence in school integration, the South opposed the move by 53 percent to 36 percent, while the whole United States favored the dispatch of troops 64 percent to 26.[11]

STUDENTS' VIEWS ON INTEGRATION

The high school polls taken by Purdue University and summarized by Dr. Martin Hamburger of New York University indicated a third of youngsters, the country over, opposed to integration.[2] "Girls generally showed more liberal attitudes than boys on racial issues." Sixty-nine percent of girls, to 58 percent of high school boys, endorsed the statement: "The morals of white students would not be lowered if they went to the same schools as Negroes."

The inevitability of integration was reflected in the Purdue polls where about 60 percent of high school students from the South, and 80 percent from other parts of the country, believed "we must eventually end segregation in the public schools."

Hamburger reported some interesting correlations in the Purdue figures. Students who favored integration rejected curbs on free speech by a four-to-one margin, and were more optimistic than the average about the chances for world peace. Students opposed to integration were relatively pessimistic about achieving a peaceful world. "This coincidence," he said, "is far beyond accident or chance."

A survey of young people, 14 to 22, in 1961, showed 22 percent of white youngsters in the South approving integration in the schools, against 65 percent of white youngsters not in the South approving—a ratio of three to one.[12]

In summary, the polls indicate that the South is still strongly opposed to integration but the opposition is diminishing here and there, while the "inevitability" of the change is beginning to command majorities.

FREEDOM OF RELIGION

In line with free speech and free press, the First Amendment in the Bill of Rights guarantees freedom of religion. We need no polls to prove that compared with colonial times, and the early days of the Republic, religious intolerance in this country has declined. Church membership per thousand of tne population is at an all-time high, but where are the bitter and sometimes bloody conflicts between Protestant and Catholic, between Christian and Jew, between various Protestant sects? We remember the ostracism of Roger Williams, the flight of the Mormons into the desert after the mob murder of their leader, Joseph Smith, the long agony of anti-Semitism—which has not ended by any means but is declining. And now the country has elected its first Catholic President. True, the election was very close, but it shows how far America has come since the defeat of Al Smith in 1928.

Question: "Are you ready to vote for a candidate for President who is a Catholic if he is well qualified?" [13]

	June 1960	Sept. 1961
Yes, I am ready	71%	82%
I am not ready	20	13
D.K.	9	5
	100	100

Prejudiced voters in these Gallup polls declined sharply after they had watched the tangible behavior of a Catholic

President. But even before Mr. Kennedy's nomination, 71 percent of adult Americans said they were ready to vote for a qualified candidate even though a Catholic.

Back in 1940, 62 percent of us said we would vote for a Catholic for President; in 1958 the figure had risen to 68 percent; in 1959 to 69 percent; and now to 82 percent. The poll takers seem to have established a steady growth of tolerance in this department.

In 1961, Gallup asked if respondents would vote for a Jew for President if he, too, were well qualified.[13] The result shows the educational spectrum again. College people voted 83 percent "Yes," high schoolers 73 percent "Yes," grade schoolers 55 percent "Yes"—still a majority. How far this vote reflects what people thought was the right and decent thing to say, in contrast with their inner prejudices, would take a series of depth interviews to determine. When Marie Jahoda conducted depth interviews in New York some years ago, anti-Semitism was found stronger underneath than on the surface by many percentage points.

A study made of a panel composed of 1,700 families, dealing with their voting behavior in the 1960 presidential election, elicited this conclusion: [14] "Protestant Democrats are more likely to act as Democrats than as Protestants, and Catholic Republicans were more likely to act as Republicans than as Catholics, in making their final choice at the polls." Party loyalty surpassed loyalty to religion when it came to voting.

Robin M. Williams, Jr., has used opinion research in an attempt to discover the ultimate values in which

Americans believe.[15] What is our operating ethic? What common set of ideas, rituals, symbols, do we cherish? What is the heart of our credo? He defines an "ultimate value" as something a person becomes intolerant about if it is challenged—something considered true by definition, and so beyond argument.

We are not, says Williams, *intolerant about our religion,* most of us. We disapprove discrimination because of a person's faith, we favor keeping church and state separate, and allowing our neighbors to follow whatever gods they choose, or no gods at all if they choose. This, he says, "is a sign that the crucial values of our system are no longer couched in a religious framework." Tolerance, Williams suggests, may be undesirable in religious matters, and his point emphasizes the difference in kind between deep religious conviction and secular opinion.

On balance, the polls show Americans favoring the principles of the Bill of Rights, often faltering in the specific application of these principles, but gradually drawing closer to the ideal—significantly so in freedom of religion, reluctantly so in freedom and equality for the races.

11
PERSONAL PROBLEMS

When people are asked in a poll what they worry about, personal problems always lead the list. Stouffer's survey in the middle fifties brings this out clearly and accurately, his two independent polling organizations double-checking each other.[1]

Question: "What kinds of things do you worry about *most*?" A list of choices was offered, and the two samples comprised 4,933 respondents. Percentages add to more than 100 because some people gave more than one answer.

Personal financial problems	43%
Health problems	24
Other personal	30
Total personal and family	97
International problems, war, etc.	8
Civil liberties, U.S. Communists, etc.	1
Other national problems	6
"Never worry"	9
Total, including multiple answers	121

Screening out the multiple answers, Stouffer concludes: "Eighty percent of the men and women in the cross-section answered solely in terms of personal and family problems." International problems, including war, national problems including unemployment and civil liberties, were well down the list. About one respondent out of 10 claimed that he, or she, never worried—but some of these may have been defending their egos. Financial worries led the personal list; health worries were high; marriage, children, in-laws, sex, completed the personal tabulation. Here are some individual replies reported by Stouffer:

Furnace maker, Michigan: "How to make a living for my family is my biggest worry. We've got the new house now if we can ever get it paid for. I don't worry about things like politics, because we have people who are paid to do that kind of worrying."

Wife of fish-hatchery owner, Georgia: "My children. They are too ambitious for our income; they take more money than we've got."

Wife of shipping clerk, New Jersey: "Paying bills. My husband has been in the hospital and may have to go back again."

Coal miner, Pennsylvania: "I worry about my pension. Might not have enough to eat. Hard times now and no work."

Farmer, Texas: "It appears that I can't prosper at nothing I do."

Schoolteacher, California: "My marriage difficulties. I have just divorced my husband."

Wife of factory worker, Wisconsin: "I worry about getting pregnant again. My doctor tells me not to worry but I do."

Wife of factory worker, Washington: "In-law troubles worry me most. Just trying to keep peace in the family and get along with my daughter-in-law."

Salesman, Illinois: "I worry most about my children getting hurt some day driving in the traffic we have on the highways."

All other polls which I have seen confirm Stouffer. I suspect that a poll on bomb shelters today would be motivated primarily by personal and family protection, only secondarily as a deterrent for nuclear war, or as a move to preserve the continuity of the nation after attack.

Look, in early 1960, found that the big worries were precisely those found by Stouffer: family finance, personal health, family troubles.[2] Fear of nuclear war was well down the table; traffic jams and nasty neighbors still further down. The type who worried most was a farmer, over 50 years of age, living in the Midwest, with only grade school education. The type who worried least was a college graduate, under 30, living in the far West.

When asked what gave the greatest satisfactions in life, the reply was usually connected with some *person*—"the man I love". . ."our four children". . ."being a grandfather." Plans for the year ahead were chiefly concerned with the family—"sending Jim to college". . ."paying off the mortgage". . ."buying one of those station wagons."

The University of Michigan reported in the same year,

1960, that money and material things accounted for half the total in one survey of worries.[3] Then came personal health, and family difficulties other than financial. Only 12 percent worried about national or world problems. The top worriers were, in order: men clerks, wives of unskilled laborers, farmers.

Earlier, in 1954, Gallup found that the worries of almost two-thirds of a nation-wide sample revolved around personal and family matters; community, national, and international matters trailed far behind.[4]

Confirmation appears again in a novel study conducted by Franklin P. Kilpatrick of National Analysts, for the Inwood Institute in 1957. One hundred Americans were interviewed, divided into five groups of 20 persons each—Negroes, immigrants, farmers, junior executives, college teachers. Each person was asked to rate the impact on himself of five kinds of problems, on a scale from 1 to 10. If the impact was severe, he rated it 10; if it was very light he rated it 1. The five problems were (1) personal, (2) family, (3) local community, (4) national U.S., (5) international. The conclusions of the study were as follows:

1. For the Negro group, personal problems scaled 10, family 9, community 7, national 6, world 2—a curve descending smoothly with the distance from the respondent's personal life.

2. Immigrants followed the same descending scale, except that world problems jumped to an impact of 7. This suggested that immigrants were still considerably involved with the old country.

3. The farm group tended to reject involvement with all problems, none rating higher than 6.

4. Junior executives ranked "personal" at 9, which could indicate deep concern with climbing the ladder of success.

5. College teachers ranked national and world problems relatively high, indicating a good imagination, along with their Ph.D.'s.

All groups scaled personal problems as their greatest concern.

Adding the scales for the five classes gave a rough measure of relative anxiety for the whole group of 100 respondents:

Personal problems	41 points
Family	35
Local community	24
National	25
World	19

Rating my own concerns on the Kilpatrick scale, I find that community, national and world problems outrank both personal and family, indicating that I am something of a deviant. The reasons, however, are fairly obvious. I have reached an age where I am no longer much concerned with getting on in the world; my financial condition is modestly secure; my health is good and my family is behaving pretty well. Meanwhile, I am writing about national and world problems, and they often keep me awake at night. Finally, as a member of the Planning Commission of my rural town, I find the community problems of zoning, subdivisions, school sites, state highways, preserving open spaces, a continuous and often exceedingly worrisome concern.

Throughout history and prehistory according to the anthropologists, the family, normally monogamous, has been the sturdiest of all human institutions. In recent years in America there has been much concern about high divorce rates, wayward children, working mothers, and the general disintegration of the family. Recent surveys, however, show a definite tendency in the opposite direction. The evidence is various and persuasive. It includes:

1. The widespread migration into single family houses in the suburbs—well documented by the 1960 U.S. Census.

2. A lower average age at marriage.

3. Fewer single persons, relatively.

4. The do-it-yourself movement, following the decline of domestic help.

5. Television in the home, competing strongly with local bars, movies and outside entertainment.

6. A shorter work week, which tends to increase time spent with the family.

Professor Ronald Freedman, University of Michigan sociologist, sums it up: [5] "With all its loss of functions, the family in a highly mobile, specialized society continues to have a unique set of core functions. It is the only social unit which can provide dependably the emotional support and stable orientation man needs in a kaleidoscopic, mobile, specialized world."

A sample of 731 housewives in the Detroit area, and 171 farm wives in Michigan, in 1960, concluded that "American marriages are not about to collapse. . . . Only a few couples are chronically unable to settle disagreements." [6] Money is the worst troublemaker, the survey shows. The chief conflict about children concerns discipline. More education tends to strengthen marriage; it improves communication between husband and wife and causes more family problems to be settled by joint decision. Cultural similarity in education and religion helps to make a successful marriage, and so does a moderate number of children. The higher the man's economic standing, the poll takers report, the better husband he is likely to make. (This correlation may or may not represent cause and effect.)

Asked what were the most valued aspects of marriage, these 902 women respondents cited four, in this order:

1. Companionship. "Doing things together."
2. The opportunity to have children.
3. "Understanding" between husband and wife.
4. Love-making.

To "understand" is a semantic umbrella. Apparently most respondents meant by it the ability to turn to one's husband for help in time of trouble. Most of them also said they were not disappointed with love-making—but would they admit it if they were? These housewives desired at least two children; many were in favor of three or four. "Wanting *one* child was as rare as wanting none."

The least satisfied wives were those who rated "companionship" as low—the husband deeply involved in his business, she lonely at home. College alumnae were the most satisfied group, claiming a high rate of mutual understanding and companionship. One might reasonably conclude from this Michigan survey of housewives that the promise of close companionship is a better augury for happy marriage than romantic love.

Another Michigan study, based on a sample of 3,000 adults in 1961, found the family breadwinner opposed to having older relatives in the home by a vote of five to one.[7] Those most financially able to support the old folks were the most opposed. Attitudes toward financial responsibility for the aged, expressed by all respondents, were:

Relatives should be primarily responsible	30%
Relatives should be solely responsible	29
Government should be solely responsible	21
Government should share with relatives	9
Government should be primarily responsible	6
D.K.	5
	100

The traditional pattern of family responsibility was still strong, but the alternative of social security was beginning to appear.

The *Look* survey found three-quarters of us "very happy" in our home life, and the same ratio said they would certainly, or probably, marry the same spouse.

Only three percent admitted they were unhappily married—probably an underestimate. Four out of five of us like where we live; 11 percent would move to California; eight percent to Florida. Sixty-five percent of us would like to travel more.

Three percent of young people in the *Look* survey would like to visit Russia, but only one percent of adults. Most youngsters think everyone should be married by 25. If they had all the money they wanted, most youngsters would:

> 1. Take a trip.
> 2. Buy a sports car, and
> 3. A big house in California, and
> 4. Settle down and raise a family.

About half of the girls said they wanted at least four children.

Let us check the *Look* report with another youth survey, also conducted by Gallup, some two years later for the *Saturday Evening Post*.[8] The nation-wide sample included 3,053 young people between 14 and 22, in high school, college, and at work. It included all levels of family income, occupation and education. Total boys and girls were about equal.

The majority wanted to marry early, at 23 or so, but after leaving college. They wanted two or three children, and a spouse who was "affectionate, sympathetic, considerate, and moral." The characteristics of intelligence, curiosity and ambition in a spouse were seldom mentioned. They wanted a little ranch house, a new but not expensive car, a job with a big company, and the chance to watch television every evening after the children were in bed. Speaking of the new car, more than half of the college boys, and the boys at work, had had a motor accident while at the wheel.

The report concludes that American youngsters have few frustrations, and are not likely to rebel or join crusades. They expect nuclear war but the prospect does not worry them greatly. They have a high regard for education, chiefly to improve the family income. Three-quarters of them believe in God "very firmly," and they believe in the hereafter. They are lenient about payola on the radio, and "cribbing" in school. The majority favor "going steady" as a principle, but only 20 percent practice it. More girls than boys claim they practice it, which creates a statistical hiatus, though the reason is not hard to locate. Nearly 70 percent say they turn first to the family when they are in trouble. "I am close to my parents."

As a group they are more liberal than conservative in politics. Nelson Rockefeller is four times as popular as Barry Goldwater, Richard Nixon three times as popular. Goldwater rates a poor third as a presidential candidate, attracting only 12 percent of young people. "As of now [late 1961] there is no conservative surge in U.S. colleges, or anywhere else among American youth." The flat statistical finding demolishes a good many recent large generalizations—possibly the result of wishful thinking—and assigns a minor role to the group unkindly nicknamed "the young fogies."

Hyman and Sheatsley, in their 1950 summary of polls, reported traditional beliefs about the family to be strongly in evidence at the time. Large majorities of adults favored absolute obedience to parents, and feared that modern children were granted too much freedom. Almost half of respondents thought prison too good for sex offenders. About a third believed that divorce laws are not strict enough. Such Draconian patterns have a suspicious sound. Were they proclaimed because they were considered the proper thing to say?

Eleven years later the attitude toward divorce was more lenient when it came to a specific case. After Nelson Rockefeller announced his marital separation in the fall of 1961, Gallup asked this question: "Suppose a candidate for President is divorced. If well qualified, would it make any difference in your voting?" Eighty-one percent said that it would not make a difference; 14 percent said it would; five percent didn't know.

MENTAL HEALTH

The nation-wide survey of 2,500 families, conducted by the Michigan Research Center and cited earlier in connection with people's worries, produced some significant figures on mental health.[3] The Great Depression, it appears, still leaves its mark in mental depression. Tension on the job, death of a loved one, fear of cancer and other diseases, were reported as frequent causes of nervous breakdown.

Fourteen percent of respondents said they had used some form of professional help, in this order:

Clergyman or priest consulted
Regular doctor
Psychiatrist, psychologist, or
    marriage counselor

Marriage counselors, respondents said, provided the least help. Lawyers were consulted only about divorce.

The survey concluded that there was "a vast unmet need" for psychiatric help, especially in the low-income group. Mental health services are more available to the higher income brackets and the better educated. "The psychologically rich get richer, the poor poorer." This study provides another striking example of how the polls can be used to improve therapy.

BIRTH CONTROL

The polls confirm the almost universal practice of birth control in American families—admitted in spite of a natural reserve toward a stranger at the door with a notebook.

The Rockefeller Foundation and the Scripps Foundation, in 1959, helped to finance a study of 2,700 American married women.[9] They were all living with their husbands, and all within the child-bearing age, 18 to 39. Five out of six partially or completely planned their families. "Nearly all consider two to four children ideal." Eighty percent use some form of contraceptives; only six percent intended never to use them. The major reasons given for planned parenthood were:

1. To allow more money for care and education of the children.

2. To protect the health of the mother.

3. To space the children so they would receive adequate attention.

4. To insure a happier family life, with children who were wanted, not resented.

Of this sample of 2,700 women, 62 percent expressed unqualified approval of contraceptives.[10] Nine percent had been surgically sterilized; seven percent were naturally sterile. "All major strata of the population," says the report, "are now using, or expect to use, some method of family limitation." This would include, presumably, the rhythm method recommended by the Catholic Church.

ATTITUDES TOWARD SEX

A Gallup poll in 1936 asked a question about venereal disease, with the expectation that doors might be slammed on their interviewers. Not at all; most respondents were quite willing to talk about it. They thought the subject should be brought into the open. When the first Kinsey report came out in 1948, only 11 percent in a survey reported by Hyman and Sheatsley said it was a "bad thing."

But in 1960, *Look* found that most Americans believed sex to be overemphasized in movies, books, magazines, and television, with movies the worst offender.[2] This was probably a cultural reaction—that is, the proper attitude to take, rather than the respondents' real feeling. If they really frowned on this display, why did they go en masse to the movies, buy the books—say, *Peyton Place*—and the salacious magazines?

A Roper poll in 1959 asked: "Do you think it is all right for either or both parties to a marriage to have had previous sexual experience?" The replies came back: [10]

It is all right to have sexual experience before marriage	22%
It is all right for the man only	8
It is not all right	54
D.K.	10
Refused to answer	6
	100

Roper found little difference between old and young respondents. The Middle West was the most puritanical region, the Northeast the most liberal. "Refused to answer" at only six percent is significant. A poll in 1899, or even 1939, might have found a majority refusing to answer such a frank question.

ATTITUDES TOWARD RELIGION

What religious credos do Americans hold, and how strongly? The very word credo, "I believe," implies religion. An anthropologist studying a strange culture pays great attention to religious belief, or, in his professional vocabulary, the "belief system" of the society. It tends to ramify and penetrate all levels of behavior, and often will explain some otherwise incomprehensible custom.

The function of a religion, in this view, is to supply a meaning for the mysteries of life and death, nature and the universe, and help people to cope with them. In the

words of C. Lloyd Warner: "All societies adjust their
members to the unknown—those forces which technology
cannot explain or control sufficiently to offer the individual
safety. Religion and magic with myth and ritual are the
accredited methods for accomplishing this fearful task."

In a sophisticated society such as ours, science and technology have lifted many former mysteries out of the dark
area of the unknown. We do not need to explain thunder
as the anger of Zeus, nor try to cure appendicitis by incan-
tation. Yet many fundamental forces remain unknown,
some probably unknowable.

In the preceding chapter we reported on religious
liberty and tolerance, under Article I of the Bill of Rights.
Now let us look at the more personal aspect.

According to the *Look* survey, 53 percent of Americans
go to church three or more times a month; another 20
percent go once or twice a month. Twenty-six percent go
seldom or never. Thus about three-quarters of us claim to
be regular churchgoers; one quarter do not. Almost all
respondents, 97 percent, said they believed in God. *Look*,
however, found little evidence of a deep religious revival
in the country.

These findings are strongly supported by Will Herberg
in a summary of polls concerned with religious beliefs.[11]
A survey in the 1950's showed that 97 percent of respondents believed in God—agreeing exactly with *Look* above.
Another study showed 96 percent; still another, 95 percent. Seventy-five percent of Americans regard themselves
as church members—again in close agreement with *Look*.

Ninety percent say that "they pray on various occasions." A majority believes in life after death and in heaven and hell. Americans think highly of the church and its ministers. They hold the Bible to be an inspired book, "the word of God." A large majority think that children should be given religious instruction, and brought up as church members.

Thus all careful polls report that most Americans are devout Christians (or Jews), holding religion to be of primary importance in their way of life. "Yet," observe Bredemeir and Toby, "these indications are after all relatively superficial." [12] They tell us what Americans believe about themselves, or what they feel they *ought* to believe. They do not tell us what their religious views really are. Nowhere are surface appearances more deceptive. Two polls effectively demonstrate this. The authors quote one trustworthy survey, in which 73 percent of respondents said they believed in life after death, with God as Supreme Judge.[13] *Only five percent, however, expressed any fear of hell.* In the old-time religion, hell was an ever-present threat, causing more anxiety, one suspects, than the looming danger of nuclear war in people's minds today.

In another dependable poll, 80 percent of respondents admitted that they were more intent upon living as comfortably as possible, here and now, than upon preparing themselves for a life hereafter. What would Calvin and Luther say to such a sentiment?

A Cornell group of social scientists in the early 1950's conducted an intensive survey of 5,000 college students.[13]

It was financed by the Carnegie Corporation, and included among the colleges Cornell, Dartmouth, Fisk, Texas, Howard, Michigan, North Carolina, California, Wayne, Wesleyan, Yale. Here is the scientists' conclusion about religious beliefs among the students interviewed:

> They are, they say, virtually all believers. Yet we find no support for any contention that campuses are seeing a revival of religion. On the contrary, we find a relative absence of commitment. . . . In religion, as in politics, students "play it cool." The content of their beliefs is decidedly away from orthodoxy . . . individualistic and relativistic approaches to religion are characteristic. Most students are agreed on the importance of religious values which appear to represent some least common denominator of personal belief. Yet when we trace some of the links between religious beliefs and social attitudes, we find certain patterns of thought which suggest that religious belief, for many students, seems to be in the service of their psychological quest for certainty. . . .

All careful surveys show that most Americans are not religious in the old-time sense, despite the devoted work of a Billy Sunday or a Billy Graham.

A fundamental principle of Christianity is "Love thy neighbor," and a survey in 1950 tested it as follows: [14]

"Which of the four statements on this card do you agree with most?"

People are good	31%
More good than bad	58
More bad than good	8
People are bad	1
D.K.	2
	100

Most Americans clearly do not agree with the sour old gentleman who was frozen in a cake of ice in a famous cartoon as he exclaimed: "People are no damn good!" Americans apparently have faith in the human race.

Millions of us are searching for "peace of mind," for mental health, by means of Christian Science, New Thought, Zen Buddism, psychoanalysis; we pursue "positive thinking," which I suspect is closer to confidence in one's ego than to confidence in God. "As we lose faith in the old religions, we look for lesser shrines."

The old faiths are losing their grip, but the "fearful task" of adjusting members of a society to the unknown is more challenging than ever.

12
THE HARD PROFILE

In the course of making this study I have examined various summaries of opinion surveys, like that of Hyman and Sheatsley, and hundreds of individual polls in detail. Out of this mass of percentages, majorities, minorities, "don't knows," high and low intensities of feeling, depth interviews, have emerged certain results that appear both long lasting and significant for an understanding of the belief systems of Americans. The results, of course, represent no complete American credo, but indicate important parts of it.

I have tried to allow for the inadequate data of a young science, and for my personal bias. Here and there I have noted with distress, or even dismay, how far my fellow citizens depart from my own views, but I have sought to report these departures objectively.

In this final chapter, I shall sketch the hard, enduring profile as it seemed to emerge from the welter of statistics. Also in this summary, with your permission, I shall introduce a few personal predilections, plainly marked, and a few suggestions for making the polls still more useful at this critical time.

The findings, I am afraid, tend to corroborate certain disparaging generalizations about Americans. They show us as frequently materialistic, shallow, and ignorant—not stupid, but uninformed in many areas, even in some areas that vitally concern our welfare. They show examples, too, of intuitive good judgment, fairness, and generosity. Lacking comparable statistics for other societies, or other times, we cannot say with certainty that contemporary Americans are more wrapped up in their own comfort and personal problems than contemporary Egyptians, for instance, or twelfth century Indonesians, or even the Periclean Greeks. When opinion research gives us at least one comparable set of reliable findings, it will furnish a clue to how much of the "apathy," the "conformity," and the "privatism" here disclosed is mid-twentieth-century American, how much is universally human. But even without a basis of comparison, this evidence can, I think, help leaders who are trying to plan legislation, mass communication, and education in their many forms.

Let us now review the major findings of this study.

FOREIGN POLICY AND ONE WORLD

Isolationism, as a government policy and a popular goal, ended 20 years ago with the Japanese attack on Pearl Harbor. The figures cited in Chapter 3 indicate that it is unlikely to return. In my opinion, if isolationism should return, as a result of continuing frustration and crisis, it could not prevail for long. Applied science has now woven

the whole planet into one technological complex, which
tightens every day. Engineers are in sight of controlling
the weather in areas outside their own nation, while some
40 satellites are now in orbit, oblivious of national bound-
aries. Any expectation that the United States government,
or popular opinion, might long exclude itself from such
technological realities is highly improbable.

The most important policy for the nation, say the majority of Americans in almost every responsible poll since
Hiroshima, is the prevention of nuclear war. We are none
too sure how it can be prevented, but we are reasonably
sure that if it comes our chances of personal survival are
dim. Four out of five of us fear terrible destruction, and
are dubious about being alive at the end of it. Until the
Berlin crisis of 1961, however, the fear was more in our
heads than in our central nervous systems.

We are not unwilling to fight if first attacked by an
enemy, but we vote heavily for negotiation as preferable
to fighting. If a fight begins with conventional weapons,
we are pretty sure it will escalate into atomic weapons. Sometimes we think that war with Russia can be
avoided, but the percentages are close, and shift with the
news. College graduates are more sanguine than the rest
of us about this. Most of us believe there will be another
world war some time—in five years, 10 years—and when
interviewers ask why, the stock reply is: "We've always
had wars and always will." This seems somewhat inconsistent with the earlier attitude, and suggests that the stock
repliers have not yet grasped the awful significance of
$E = MC^2$.

Most Americans were not disposed to fight for the off-shore islands, Quemoy and Matsu, in the crisis in the Formosa straits several years ago, and were not disposed to overthrow Castro in Cuba by force in 1961. Only if Russia attempted to establish a military base in Cuba would we favor sending in the Marines. Cuba, we think, is a job for the Organization of American States and the United Nations. We are still, at latest accounts, strongly opposed to recognizing Red China diplomatically, or admitting her to membership in the United Nations. If, however, the U.N. some day votes to admit China, we vote to play along.

Ever since the United Nations was organized in 1945, heavy majorities of Americans have favored it in principle; the pull-out vote has never risen above 13 percent. Satisfaction with the U.N.'s performance, however, shifts with the news. We want the U.N. to settle all manner of disputes—Berlin, Formosa, Cuba, the Suez Canal, the Congo, outer space—most of which its present machinery is not adequate to cope with. But we stubbornly continue to reach out our hands for an agency above and beyond our own country to rescue us from nuclear wars and disasters.

Sample polls of *Who's Who in America,* of members of the American Bar Association, of voters in a New Jersey Congressional district, all unite in demanding that the United States *take the lead* in preparing plans for a durable peace. This contrasts with frequent statements from Washington—in my personal observation—to the effect that if disaster comes "you must blame the Russians." These three sets of respondents seem to be asking for an American leader who will say: "If peace comes, you can blame me."

Most of us vote repeatedly for disarmament with inspection and control. We distrust Russia profoundly, and think Mr. Khrushchev is "bluffing" when he asks for complete disarmament. This to me reflects another tragic situation. I visited Russia in the summer of 1961 in connection with a cultural exchange program. I met a number of leading scientists, writers, academicians, philosophers, who, to a man, feared war. Most of them had lost members of their family in the last war; all of them had struggled to rebuild Russia after Hitler had wrecked vast areas of it. I became convinced that Russians not only want disarmament, but badly need it. Military expenditures, I was told on high authority, now take at least a quarter of the gross national product. The Russians I met, including some military experts, seemed sure that a nuclear war could not be won; they agreed with their scientists that the result would be nearer to mutual suicide.

If most Americans and most Russians truly want disarmament, there ought to be some way for leaders to come to terms.* The Kremlin, I believe, has been clumsy and stupid in its attempts to achieve a deeply felt goal of the Russian people.

THE BUSINESS SYSTEM

The polls show that the appeal of "Communism" in America is nonexistent today, and that the appeal of

---

* A thoughtful plan of action has been sketched by Grenville Clark and Louis B. Sohn in *World Peace Through World Law*. Harvard University Press, 1960.

"Socialism" is at an all-time low. There was some sentiment for democratic socialism in the Great Depression of
the 1930's, but it has evaporated. Most of us want no part
of anything by that name.

Most of us want no part, either, of anything called the
"welfare state." But when interviewers ask about the de-
sirability of social security, public housing, federal aid to
schools, medical care for the aged, we usually favor these
proposals by large majorities. We are hazy on economic
definitions, and do not often find the referents for abstract
terms like "welfare state" or "free enterprise."

There is some ideological objection to "bigness" as such,
but Americans no longer worry much about monopoly
and Big Business—indeed, Big Labor worries them more.
Respondents are pleased when a son gets a job with a large
corporation, but two-thirds of us, when we get right down
to it, would rather be our own boss than work for a big
firm.

Interesting things are happening to the attitudes of consumers in recent years. Folklore about the sinfulness of
going into debt is softening under the temptations of buying on the installment plan. Instead of a resulting decline
in thrift and savings, however, factual surveys show the
reverse to be nearer the truth. Individual savings are at
an all-time high. A similar effect appears to have followed
social security legislation. Instead of causing people to
lean on the state, as widely and ominously predicted, the
legislation has apparently made most Americans security
conscious, and stimulated them to increase their personal
savings.

Inflation may worry the financial community, but most Americans take it in stride. It is a problem, yes, but what goes up, we think, must come down.

The American middle class, with income between $5,000 and $10,000 a year, is the chief pace setter for new products and gadgets in the nation—a phenomenon unprecedented in history. "In the past few decades, many new and generally accepted ways of living have started outside upper-class homes," says a University of Michigan survey.

However weak we may be on economic theory, most of us no longer believe that depressions are inevitable, like hurricanes and floods. We believe that another 1929 is impossible; government action through public works and other measures will prevent it. The government, we also believe, can help maintain full employment. Thus we accept a "mixed economy," where government, business, and labor cooperate in an open society.

WORK

The majority of Americans have been in favor of labor unions for a generation. The percentage of approval shifts with strikes in the news, but never falls below 50 percent on a nation-wide basis. Featherbedding is something else again—jail is none too severe for offenders, according to some polls. Compulsory arbitration is widely favored, and so is the minimum wage law raising base pay to more than one dollar an hour.

The polls disclose a paradoxical attitude toward one's job in our high-energy society. On the surface, majorities usually say they like their work. But below the surface, a number of careful depth interviews have found quite otherwise. Only one man in 10 is happy—or at least not unhappy—working on the assembly line. The other nine like the pay and the fringe benefits, but hate the monotony, repetition, and inability to use their minds. "The job is so sickening day in and day out plugging in ignition wires. I get through one motor, turn around, and there's another motor staring me in the face. . . ." "The only satisfaction around here, Doc, is the old buck."

A careful study of attitudes toward automation in clerical work indicates a similar dissatisfaction. Office workers need less intelligence, as minor decisions are handed over to electronic computers. White-collar workers, along with blue collars, report that they are losing the sense of responsibility as automation gains. Meanwhile satisfaction for professional workers tends to increase. Blue collars on the assembly line, in their solitary maneuvers with another motor staring them in the face, suffer also from the loss of teamwork, so essential to job satisfaction.

POLITICS

Homo Americanus is not a political animal. His involvement, when it comes, usually takes the form of "Who's going to win?" He tends to put an election on a par with the World Series in baseball. The task of the voter, as the voter sees it, is to select leaders, not policies. "I pay taxes to let the politicians do the worrying."

The typical voter has joined the party of his father by the time he is 30, but believes there is little to choose between the Democrats and Republicans. He hopes that his son will not go into politics; a job with the Telephone Company is much to be preferred. Here we encounter another curious paradox, for at the same time the polls show that he thinks highly of Presidents, Senators, Justices of the Supreme Court (unless he is from the South), Cabinet members, Governors, and even Mayors of large cities. These official posts have high status, but he hopes his children will avoid office-holding as a career.

Most Americans do not follow the four rules of classic political science in their voting behavior. They do *not* take a strong interest in politics; they do *not* know much about most political issues; they do *not* act on rigorous political principles; their political behavior is *not* guided by logic and reason. After this conclusion, which must reduce Locke, Burke and Bentham to posthumous despair, the famous Elmira study goes on to show that if voters *did* follow these four political imperatives, American democracy might be unworkable. We would become so fiercely political that election day could be the occasion for a massacre. We need, the study shows, a certain amount of apathy to keep democracy healthy. Another careful study, covering voting behavior in New Haven, Connecticut, confirms the Elmira conclusion. The United States has evolved a kind of political mulch in which democracy seems to thrive. At least so far.

The polls show there is now little difference between the attitudes of rural and urban voters on political questions. One would expect this—as power lines, electric conveniences, television, and station wagons invade the farms.

The farm bloc in Congress retains much of its power as a vested interest, but its base is weakening.

A reliable system of opinion research would be a great help to an American President in his basic task of communication with the people. It could tell him not only what solid majorities want and what they fear, but perhaps even more important, what they *don't know*. It could identify areas of public ignorance, and so tell the President what to clarify in his next fireside chat.

EDUCATION

Education is a fundamental tenet in the American credo. We are all for it. If we have children we are hoping to send them to college, and are saving money to that end. One careful poll shows the best teacher in town outranking the best lawyer, the best businessman, or best public official in popular respect. The teacher even outranks the best clergyman, except among the Negro group. We vote heavily in favor of federal aid to schools. When asked what changes we would make if we lived our lives over again, the first answer is "more education."

This is all very fine, but what do Americans hope from more education? Is it knowledge, wisdom, a better understanding of the world and of themselves? Alas no, only a tiny minority desires that. Most of us want more education to enable us to earn more money. "A college education," concludes a Roper poll in 1959, "is now more widely regarded for its economic and status values than for the intellectual training it is supposed to afford." The popular goal is not so much to accumulate a fortune, as to assure a comfortable family life surrounded with all the latest artifacts.

Our educational system absorbs billions of dollars and millions of lives, but it apparently does not show students how to relate their lives and occupations to the community around them. We are so preoccupied in adapting to material change that we hardly notice where the changes are taking us.

The popular indifference to educational content is corroborated by all surveys which deal with the reading of books. Three out of five adult Americans in a recent study admitted that they had not read any book—except possibly the Bible—during the previous year. Comparative surveys show Britons reading three times as many books per person as Americans; Germans and Australians twice as many; Canadians almost twice as many. Compared with the time the average American spends before his television set, the time he spends reading books is minuscule. There are, however, books and books; perhaps more detective stories, comics and Westerns would not make us any wiser.

One offset will occur immediately to the reader of this book. He will have noted poll after poll where the evidence is plain that the more years a respondent spends in school, the more tolerant he is likely to be and the better his judgment. However materialistic our educational goals may be, and however limited our reading, something happens to our mental processes in school which makes us better citizens. As nearly all signs point to more schooling for Americans in the years ahead, especially in college, one may logically expect an increasingly mature electorate.

SCIENCE

Before the Russians launched Sputnik I, the popular image of a scientist in America was anything but flattering. Many high school students in a famous poll pictured him as a "longhair," a "brain," slightly mad and possibly dangerous. Recently the image has improved. He is now "working for the common good" and quite sane and dependable.

While we respect science, however, most of us cannot define it. We confuse the scientific method with "hard study," and have little conception of hypothesis, verification, prediction and controlled experiment. We have little conception of the distinction between pure science, as illustrated by the formula $E = MC^2$, and applied science, as illustrated by the antimissile missile. When asked where more scientific research is especially needed, most respondents rate medicine first. Putting a man on the moon comes far down the list—or did before the orbiting of Colonel John Glenn.

Polls show that we are none too sure the scientific method can be applied to problems of human behavior, though many of us would like to see it tried in the field of juvenile delinquency. The idea expressed in Alexander Pope's classic phrase, that "the proper study of mankind is man," has not yet found a high place in the American credo. It seems, however, to be gaining.

CIVIL LIBERTIES

Americans are heartily in favor of "liberty" and "freedom" in principle, but percentages of approval shrink when its comes to specific situations. The abstraction ranks above performance. Free speech is fine, but a substantial minority would not allow a Socialist to hire a hall in town, or publish a newspaper. Most of us cannot name the freedoms in the Bill of Rights. A majority of high school students in a nation-wide survey said that books, movies, radio, and television should be censored "to shield us from improper thinking."

The nation is still split wide open on the question of civil liberties for Negroes. The North supports the decisions of the Supreme Court on integration in schools, trains, buses, waiting rooms; the South opposes them. It is encouraging to note, however, that the opposition is gradually lessening, while a 1961 poll shows three-quarters of adults in the Southern states ready to concede that desegregation must some day come.

We hate "Communists," but are quite unable to describe them. The Wisconsin farmer quoted earlier was probably typical. "They are no good, to my notion. I can't figure out what they are." Communists are often equated with democratic socialism—which opposes violence and revolution; they are equated with liberals, New Dealers, free traders, atheists, indeed, with anybody possessing novel or strange ideas. One small but vigorous group has attempted to impeach Mr. Justice Warren of the Supreme Court as a Communist agent—all this when as we have seen Communism has lost whatever appeal it may have had.

Near the peak of the late Senator McCarthy's career, Stouffer made a classic opinion survey, using two dependable agencies to check each other's findings. He concluded that Americans were interested in the *news* about Reds in the government, the churches, the universities, but: "the number of people who said that they were worried, either about the threat of Communists in the United States, or about civil liberties, was, by the most generous interpretation, less than one percent." The key word, of course, was "worried."

The Bill of Rights guarantees freedom of religion, including freedom not to embrace a religion. Americans accept this increasingly in their behavior. The popularity of a Catholic President has increased since he took office; a majority of respondents would vote for a Jew for President if he were well qualified.

Robin M. Williams, Jr., using the technique of opinion research, has tried to find the heart of the American credo. What are our ultimate values? An ultimate value he defines as a belief we are intolerant about if it is challenged —a belief that we consider true by definition. Most of us are not, Williams finds, intolerant about religion. We favor the separation of church and state, and would allow citizens to worship wherever they please, or nowhere if they pleased. In brief, our tolerance is much broader when it comes to religion than to race, or even economic doctrine.

PERSONAL PROBLEMS

All polls show that the personal problems of Americans outrank, by large margins, community, national and international problems—except in time of actual war. The Cold War with Russia has had little effect on the percentages. Our deepest satisfactions are personal—"the man I love," "our four children." Teen-agers when asked their goals are likely to specify a new car, a ranch house, early marriage, and a happy family. American youngsters are apathetic about politics, and do not substantiate reports of a crusade toward the extreme right. The more years of schooling we have had, the greater our concern for nonpersonal issues, but it never reaches, for most of us, the concern we feel for family, children, job, health, income, status.

Contrary to a widespread impression, the polls demonstrate that the American family as an institution is growing bigger and stronger. It raises more children than a generation ago; it contains more home-centered interests, due to television, the split-level home in the suburbs, "do-it-yourself" activities, and shorter hours of work.

The well-to-do family now has more children than the low-income family—a shift of high significance. Birth control, the polls show, is practiced by all but a small minority of Americans, and approved by most. Discussion of sex has become more open and tolerant. Most of us think some moving pictures, and some books and magazines, treat sex too broadly, but most of us go right on viewing or reading them. The most valued attribute of marriage, respondents say, is companionship.

The polls show an increase in church membership per thousand of the population, but no evidence of any deep religious revival. College students respect religion, but "play it cool." We believe, nine out of 10 of us, that people are more good than bad—which seems a sound ethical basis for a society to build upon.

FINALLY

What does this study imply about political democracy and the open society? Can it hold its own against the closed societies evolving all around us? Have the mass of the American people the will and the judgment to defend their institutions against competing systems? This is not an easy question to answer, in the light of the record. The record shows some appalling lapses in will and judgment. I think, however, we can say this: the record shows that the rank and file are sometimes ahead of their leaders. This was particularly true in the last war when people called for more planes, rationing systems, price and wage controls, forced savings—long before Congress got around to it. It is true, I think, in present attitudes toward peace, negotiation, world law, disarmament. People's judgment may improve still further as they face the grim details of civil defense.

When citizens are personally involved in issues, their reactions tend to be on the side not only of common sense but of intelligent judgment. The key to motivation is interest. If we are really interested we use that remarkable and neglected instrument, the human brain. Normal people, people in the mass, are not stupid, as some truly stupid people suppose; they are just uninterested.

Among the subjects where interest has not been aroused, and where this study shows excessive ignorance and confusion, are these:

Unawareness of the imperatives of the nuclear age.

Unawareness of the massive effects of technology on our lives, and on our future.

Unawareness of the helps to understanding available in the social sciences.

Unawareness of the true goals of education.

Indifference to the population explosion.

The paradox implicit in high regard for public office, like President and Senator, against the hope that one's children will never seek public office.

Ignorance of the Bill of Rights and what it means to a democratic society.

Little comprehension of the essential difference between open and closed societies.

Gross inability to define "Communism," and so intelligently assess its threat.

This study strongly indicates that political democracy is firmly based on a potential intelligence in most citizens, provided they are interested and informed of the issues confronting them. The task for leaders in a democracy is to locate areas of ignorance, to arouse citizens' interest in important public questions and so tap this enormous potential.

Here public opinion research can lend a powerful hand. We remember Samuel Stouffer's prophecy for the young science: "There is no turning back."

APPENDIX OF SOURCES

Sources in many chapters are so numerous that they would clutter the text, either with full descriptions, or with footnotes. So they are put here in the Appendix, with numbers for each chapter corresponding to those found in the text—usually at the end of the first sentence referring to the source.

"AIPO" refers to the American Institute of Public Opinion at Princeton, headed by Dr. George Gallup.

Public Pulse is published by Elmo Roper and Associates, who also made the surveys for *Fortune*.

"NORC" refers to the National Opinion Research Center at the University of Chicago.

Other sources are spelled out.

Though the Appendix does not always give the original source in detail, it offers the interested reader a definite reference to consult, and assures him that the text is founded upon the reports of dependable agencies at specified dates.

Chapter 1 GROWTH OF A SCIENCE

1. *The American Behavioral Scientist*, April, 1961.
2. *Journal of Social Issues*, May, 1946.
3. Samuel A. Stouffer: *The American Soldier*. Princeton University Press, 1949.
4. AIPO, Sept. 27, 1961.

Chapter 2 MEASURING OPINION

1. Herbert H. Hyman and Paul B. Sheatsley: "The Current Status of American Public Opinion." Chapter 2 in *Yearbook of the National Council for Social Studies*, 1950.
2. Reported in New York *Post*, *Oct.* 19, 1960.
3. William A. Lydgate: *What Our People Think*. Crowell, 1944.

Chapter 3 FOREIGN POLICY

1. AIPO, March 15, 1961.
2. AIPO, Sept. 16, 1959.
3. AIPO, March 23, 1958.
4. Roper, Election Study III, November, 1961.
5. NORC, Aug. 28, 1952.
6. AIPO, March 4, 1958.
7. AIPO, Feb. 1, 1961.
8. AIPO, May 14, 1958.
9. Letter to author from Irving F. Laucks.
10. Joseph T. Klapper: *The Effects of Mass Communication*. Glencoe, Illinois, Free Press, 1960.
11. AIPO, June 1, 1960.
12. AIPO, Aug. 20, 1961.
13. *New York Times*, Sept. 2, 1961.
14. AIPO, Sept. 13, 1961.
15. Buchanan, William and Hadley Cantril: *How Nations See Each Other*. University of Illinois Press, 1953.
16. AIPO, April 26, 1961.

17. Samuel A. Stouffer: *Communism, Conformity, and Civil Liberties.* Doubleday, 1955.
18. AIPO, June 19, 1960.
19. AIPO, Jan. 1, 1961.
20. AIPO, June 7, 1961.
21. AIPO, May 5, 1961.
22. AIPO, Nov. 10, 1961.
23. AIPO, July 14, 1961.
24. AIPO, July 31, 1961.
25. Gallup's German service, Nov. 19, 1961.
26. *New Leader,* Nov. 27, 1961, citing Gallup poll in France.
27. AIPO, Aug. 2, 1961.
28. AIPO, May 7, 1961.
29. AIPO, Oct. 6, 1961.
30. AIPO, May 3, 1961.
31. *Public Pulse,* Nov. 22, 1958.
32. AIPO, March 19, 1961.
33. Quoted in an editorial in *The Progressive,* October, 1961.

Chapter 4 TOWARD ONE WORLD

1. *Look,* Jan. 5, 1960.
2. Buchanan, William and Hadley Cantril: *How Nations See Each Other.* University of Illinois Press, 1953.
3. AIPO, Oct. 8, 1961.
4. William A. Scott and Stephen B. Withey: *The United States and the United Nations, The Public View, 1945-1955.* Prepared under the auspices of the Survey

Research Center, University of Michigan. Manhattan Publishing Co., 1958.

5. AIPO, Feb. 2, 1961.

6. AIPO, Sept. 1, 1961.

7. American Association for the United Nations: *News*, September, 1961.

8. AIPO, Feb. 5, 1961.

9. *Public Pulse*, September, 1959.

10. Reported in editorial, *Saturday Review*, Sept. 30, 1961.

11. *Public Pulse*, Sept. 20, 1958.

12. AIPO, September, 1961 (special release).

13. AIPO, Nov. 26, 1961.

14. AIPO, Nov. 23, 1960.

15. AIPO, Nov. 29, 1961.

Chapter 5   THE BUSINESS SYSTEM

1. *Fortune*, July, 1942.

2. *Fortune*, November, 1948.

3. Gallup Surveys #447 and #448, September, 1949.

4. *Fortune*, July, 1948.

5. *Fortune*, September, 1948.

6. Roper, Commercial report, October, 1952.

7. Gallup Survey #454, March, 1950.

8. AIPO, Sept. 9, 1961.

9. AIPO, March 8, 1961.

10. Gallup, reported in *New York Times*, May 3, 1960.

11. *Saturday Evening Post*, Dec. 30, 1961.

12. George Katona: *The Powerful Consumer*. McGraw-Hill, 1960.

13. Reported in *Look,* Jan. 5, 1960.
14. Gallup Survey #564, May, 1956.
15. Roper: *Current Topics,* April, 1945.
16. Roper, September, 1957.
17. *Public Pulse,* August, 1958.
18. *Public Pulse,* October, 1958.
19. University of Michigan News Service, April, 1961.
20. Cited by Rensis Likert of Michigan Survey Research Center in an address in 1959.
21. AIPO, Jan. 11, 1961.
22. AIPO, June 23, 1959.

Chapter 6 WORK

1. *Saturday Evening Post,* Dec. 30, 1961.
2. AIPO, May 26, 1961.
3. AIPO, Feb. 15, 1961.
4. AIPO, Jan. 5, 1959.
5. AIPO, Oct. 17, 1949.
6. AIPO, Nov. 10, 1959.
7. *Progressive,* January, 1959.
8. AIPO, March 12, 1961.
9. AIPO, Aug. 23, 1961.
10. University of Michigan News Service, Feb. 23, 1959.
11. *New York Times,* Aug. 30, 1960.
12. University of Michigan News Service, Aug. 31, 1960.
13. *Public Pulse,* August, 1957.
14. George Katona: *The Powerful Consumer.* McGraw-Hill, 1960.
15. Standard Oil Company of New Jersey. Report not published.

16. *Harvard Business Review,* November, 1958.
17. Walker and Guest: *The Man on the Assembly Line.* Harvard University Press, 1952.
18. AIPO, April 25, 1949.
19. Minnesota Poll, July, 1956.

Chapter 7   POLITICS

 1. Berelson, Lazarsfeld and McPhee: *Voting.* University of Chicago Press, 1954.
 2. Robert A. Dahl in *Science,* Oct. 27, 1961.
 3. Hyman and Sheatsley, in *Yearbook of the National Council for Social Studies.* 1950.
 4. University of Michigan News Service, March 18, 1960.
 5. *Public Pulse,* October, 1960.
 6. NORC, February, 1948.
 7. NORC, December, 1946.
 8. Campbell, Converse, Miller and Stokes: *The American Voter.* John Wiley, 1960.
 9. *Saturday Review,* Feb. 11, 1961.
10. Stephen K. Bailey: Occasional Paper for The Fund for the Republic. June, 1959.
11. AIPO, Aug. 26, 1960.
12. University of Michigan News Service, July 29, 1959.
13. Cited by Stuart Chase in *Power of Words.* Harper, 1954.
14. University of Michigan News Service, Sept. 21, 1960.
15. AIPO, March 5, 1955.
16. *Public Pulse,* December, 1958.
17. AIPO, April 9, 1961.

18. *Public Pulse,* September, 1959.
19. *Public Pulse,* May, 1959.

Chapter 8   EDUCATION

1. Speech by Roper at University of North Dakota, April 19, 1960.
2. Samuel Stouffer: *Communism, Conformity and Civil Liberties.* Doubleday, 1955.
3. Roper: Pre-Convention Survey, June, 1960.
4. Roper, August, 1950 (Commercial #40).
5. AIPO, April 14, 1961.
6. University of Michigan News Service, March 14, 1960.
7. AIPO, April 5, 1961.
8. AIPO, March 31, 1961.
9. *Time,* March 7, 1961.
10. Letter to the author, March 9, 1960.
11. *Look,* Jan. 5, 1960.
12. Harry C. Bredemeier and Jackson Toby: *Social Problems in America.* John Wiley, 1960.
13. *Public Pulse,* September, 1959.
14. F. P. Kilpatrick in *Journal of Individual Psychology.* November, 1960.
15. *Saturday Review,* June 18, 1960.
16. University of Michigan News Service, March 24, 1960.
17. AIPO, Aug. 13, 1955.
18. Report of National Book Committee, March, 1958.
19. *N.E.A. Journal,* April, 1959.
20. Lester Asheim in *Reading for Life.* University of Michigan Press, 1959.

21. *Public Pulse,* December, 1956.
22. AIPO, Oct. 17, 1953.

Chapter 9 SCIENCE

1. *New York Times,* Sept. 9, 1956.
2. New York *Herald Tribune,* Feb. 28, 1957.
3. *Time,* Feb. 3, 1958.
4. *Christian Science Monitor,* Dec. 3, 1957.
5. *New York Times,* Nov. 17, 1961.
6. University of Michigan News Service, May 15, 1959.
7. Stephen B. Withey: *Satellites, Science and the Public.* University of Michigan Press, 1959.
8. University of Michigan News Service, Feb. 27, 1959.
9. AIPO, Nov. 5, 1957.
10. Minnesota Poll, October, 1957.
11. University of Michigan News Service, Aug. 17, 1958.
12. AIPO, June 21, 1961.
13. C. P. Snow: *The Two Cultures and the Scientific Revolution.* Cambridge University Press, 1959.
14. London *Times,* Sept. 29, 1961.

Chapter 10 CIVIL LIBERTIES

1. Hyman and Sheatsley, in *Yearbook of the National Council for Social Studies.* 1950.
2. *New York Times,* Feb. 16, 1960.
3. AIPO, June 14, 1961.
4. University of Michigan News Service, April 17, 1961.
5. *Progressive,* January, 1959.
6. Samuel Stouffer: *Communism, Conformity and Civil Liberties.* Doubleday, 1955.

7. Samuel Stouffer: *The American Soldier.* Princeton University Press, 1949.

8. AIPO, Aug. 14, 1957.

9. *Public Pulse,* December, 1958.

10. *Time,* April 7, 1961.

11. AIPO, June 21, 1961.

12. *Saturday Evening Post,* Dec. 30, 1961.

13. AIPO, Sept. 24, 1961.

14. University of Michigan News Service, Aug. 30, 1961.

15. Bredemeier and Toby: *Social Problems in America.* John Wiley, 1960.

Chapter 11 PERSONAL PROBLEMS

1. Samuel Stouffer: *Communism, Conformity and Civil Liberties.* Doubleday, 1954.

2. *Look,* Jan. 5, 1960.

3. University of Michigan News Service, May 25, 1960.

4. AIPO, Sept. 11, 1954.

5. University of Michigan News Service, Aug. 31, 1959.

6. University of Michigan News Service, Sept. 21, 1960, summarizing book by Bloode and Wolfe: *Husbands and Wives.*

7. University of Michigan News Service, Oct. 13, 1961.

8. *Saturday Evening Post,* Dec. 30, 1961.

9. Whelpton, Friedman and Campbell: *Family Planning, Sterility and Population Growth.* University of Michigan Press, 1959.

10. *Public Pulse,* November, 1959.

11. Will Herberg: *Protestant, Catholic, Jew.* Doubleday, 1955.

12. Bredemeier and Toby: *Social Problems in America.* John Wiley, 1960.

13. Robin Williams *et al*: *What College Students Think.* Van Nostrand Press, 1960.

14. Roper Commercial #43, 1950.

INDEX *

* Because of the great number of references and cross references to hundreds of polls, each with its variety of items, a complete index would be almost as long as the book itself. This index is therefore confined to proper names, and to selected subjects, chiefly the subject matter appearing in the side headings of the various chapters.

About the Author

Stuart Chase has won a world-wide reputation by his skill in making important and difficult ideas clear, readable and interesting. An independent liberal in politics, Mr. Chase has had an important influence on the consumer movement, the study of semantics and communication, the policy of soil conservation (through his book *Rich Land, Poor Land*, published during the administration of Franklin Roosevelt) and on the New Deal in government itself. Many a recent college graduate looks back on Chase's books on economics and social science as a bright spot in the wasteland of academic reading; many a general reader has been introduced through his works to a new field and a new outside interest.

Born in New Hampshire, educated at M.I.T. and Harvard, Stuart Chase became a C.P.A. and entered his father's accounting firm in Boston. Soon, however, he decided that he would rather write his own books than audit the books of other people's businesses. He began writing about economics from the point of view of the consumer, and made use of his accounting experience in such works as *The Tragedy of Waste, Your Money's Worth, Idle Money, Idle Men, Where's the Money Coming From? Tomorrow's Trade,* and *The Economy of Abundance. The Tyranny of Words, Power of Words, Guides to Straight Thinking,* and *Roads to Agreement* dealt with various aspects of communication, especially on reducing disagreement and conflict. The wide range of his interest is shown in such other titles as *Mexico, Democracy Under Pressure, Some Things Worth Knowing* and *Live and Let Live.* His books have been translated into a dozen foreign languages, his *Mexico* into Braille.

Mr. Chase lives in Redding, Connecticut, where he takes an active interest in community affairs. He also spends a good deal of time caring for his tennis court, playing on it, skiing on the back hill, and practicing conservation and forestry in a small way. For an indoor hobby he sketches cats competently enough for exhibition.

Set in Linotype Caledonia
Format by Barbara Luttringhaus
Manufactured by American Book-Stratford Press
Published by HARPER & BROTHERS, *New York*